Rise and Fall

Rise and Fall

A History of the World in Ten Empires

Paul Strathern

HODDER &
STOUGHTON

First published in Great Britain in 2019 by Hodder & Stoughton
An Hachette UK company

2

A CIP catalogue record for this title
is available from the British Library

Hardback ISBN 978 1 473 69862 8
Trade Paperback ISBN 978 1 473 69863 5
eBook ISBN 978 1 473 69864 2

Typeset in Plantin Light by
Palimpsest Book Production Ltd, Falkirk, Stirlingshire

Printed and bound in Great Britain by
Clays Ltd, Elcograf S.p.A.

Hodder & Stoughton policy is to use papers that are natural,
renewable and recyclable products and made from wood grown
in sustainable forests. The logging and manufacturing processes
are expected to conform to the environmental regulations
of the country of origin.

Hodder & Stoughton Ltd
Carmelite House
50 Victoria Embankment
London EC4Y 0DZ

www.hodder.co.uk

To the Kaiser and Lenin

Contents

Introduction

Three Telling Tales of Empire

At the turn of the fifteenth century, China was by some degree the most advanced civilisation on earth. This was the land, tales of whose wonders Marco Polo had earlier brought back to Europe. In 1405, Zhu Di, third emperor of the Ming Dynasty, ordered Admiral Zheng He to set sail from China with his fleet to explore 'the oceans of the world'.

Admiral Zheng He had been in the service of the Emperor Zhu Di since he had been captured as an adolescent, and castrated according to contemporary custom. Zheng He had consequently risen through the ranks to become a man of mighty stature, both politically and physically. Eye-witness reports describe him as being almost seven feet tall and nearly five feet in girth. The fleet he commanded was of even more impressive proportions. It contained over three hundred large ocean-going, wooden-sailed junks manned by more than 28,000 men. The admiral's treasure ship, a replica of which can be seen in Nanjing today, was 450 feet long. No comparable fleet would put to sea for over four centuries, until the First World War.

Zheng He and his fleet undertook six voyages between

1405 and 1424, during the course of which he travelled from Vietnam to Indonesia, from Burma, India and Ceylon to the Persian Gulf and up the Red Sea to Jeddah, then around the Horn of Africa down as far south as Kenya. Precise records of these six voyages are no longer extant, but it seems likely that in the course of his travels, Zheng He must have covered a distance equivalent to circumnavigating the globe twice over. Amongst the many wonders that he transported back to China was a giraffe from Somalia. Its arrival in China caused a sensation, confirming the existence of the legendary Chinese *qilin*, which in the sixth century BC had foretold the arrival of 'a king without a throne': later taken to be the philosopher Confucius, whose ideas would guide China through two millennia.

In 1430, when Zheng He was in his sixtieth year, he was ordered to undertake a seventh voyage and 'to proceed all the way to the end of the earth'. This voyage would take three years, extend far into legend, and be a voyage from which he would never return. According to the controversial claims of naval historian Gavin Menzies, this voyage took Zheng He around the Cape of Good Hope to West Africa, from whence he crossed the Atlantic to America and rounded Cape Horn, sailing as far north as California. One admiral, who separated from Zheng He's main fleet, is said to have reached Greenland and returned to China by way of northern Siberia (a passage that is likely to have remained open due to the after-effects of the Medieval Warm Period). Another admiral is said to have sailed as far as Australia, New Zealand and the first drift ice of Antarctica.

Evidence for Gavin Menzies' claims are, according to

Harvard historian Niall Ferguson, 'at best circumstantial and at worst non-existent'. Despite this, tantalising anomalies appear to remain in the form of Chinese DNA discovered amongst Venezuelan native tribes, 'a number of medieval Chinese anchors . . . found off the California coast', as well as some surprisingly prescient coastal features that appeared on maps drawn prior to information received from fifteenth-century European explorers. Confirmation that Menzies' amazing claims concerning Zheng He's legendary seventh expedition were taken seriously in some quarters emerged when the Chinese president Hu Jintao addressed the Australian parliament in 2003, and asserted that 'the Chinese . . . had discovered Australia three centuries before Captain Cook.' This has now seemingly become official Chinese history.

A modern representation of Admiral Zheng He's treasure ship, alongside the vessel in which Columbus sailed the Atlantic.

In the years following Admiral Zheng He's death in India in 1433, new Confucian ministers had risen to power at court, who 'were hostile to commerce and . . . to all things foreign.' A series of Imperial Haijin Decrees (Sea Bans) were issued, forbidding Chinese ships from sailing to foreign nations. Official records of Zheng He's voyages were destroyed, and the imperial fleet was confined to port, where it soon fell into disrepair. These decrees were initially proclaimed as a measure against Japanese pirates, but had the unintended consequence of isolating China from the outside world. The progressive outgoing Ming civilisation began to ossify, and 'one of the greatest eras of orderly government and social stability in human history' fell into decline.

Our second telling tale concerning the ethos and legacy of empire happens to take place some three centuries later, just as Chinese isolation was beginning to be disturbed by the arrival of European traders, such as the Portugese, the Dutch and the British. By now, the British were beginning to impose their colonial administration on India. An exemplary instance of this took place in 1770, when the northern province of Bihar was devastated by one of its recurrent famines. Consequently, the de facto ruler of British India, Warren Hastings, ordered the construction of what became known as the Granary of Patna. Captain John Garstin, an engineer in the East India Company Army, was ordered to erect a building 'for the perpetual prevention of famine in the province'.

The result was a highly imaginative edifice, which the locals named the Golghar ('the round house'). Almost 100 feet tall and nearly 500 feet in circumference at ground level, it dominated the surrounding Indian dwellings, its summit providing views over the city of Patna to the Ganges, sacred river of the Hindus. Its dome-like structure would be recognised by the local population as resembling both a Buddhist stupa and the dome of an Islamic mosque. Ascending around the dome was a spiral staircase, for the use of Indian bearers carrying sacks of grain to be emptied through the hole in the top of the dome, gradually filling the internal hemisphere with sufficient grain to provide for any future famines. The Golghar would be judged to be 'touched . . . with the machismo of the imperial presence . . . the most famous of the practical structures of the Raj.'

Captain Garstin ordered an inscription on the side of his architectural masterpiece, which announced that it was 'First filled and publickly closed by . . .' This proclamation remained forever incomplete. According to the visiting Victorian poet Emily Eden, the Golghar 'was found to be useless'. When I visited Patna, and was shown this celebrated structure, still in good condition almost two centuries after its completion, I was informed of the reason for its redundancy. According to my guide, the door in the base of the dome, through which the grain should have poured out once it was filled, had in fact been constructed so that it only opened inwards.

Some modern sources dispute this significant detail, but when I visited Patna, I could find no one who was not adamant concerning the veracity of this incompetence, and consequent suffering, inflicted by the British. Such views may have been reinforced by the fact that many I spoke to were of sufficient age for the last Bihar famine of 1966–67 to have been more than a folk memory.

Our third tale of empire brings us into the modern times,

when as we shall see many had good reason to believe that this would be the era of humanity's last empires. The world's two great empires appeared to be hell-bent upon destroying the world itself.

In 1945 the United States' Manhattan Project under Robert Oppenheimer was in a race to complete the world's first atomic bomb. Many of the scientists working under Oppenheimer at the remote Los Alamos site in the New Mexico desert had fled Germany as a result of the Nazi decrees against the Jews, and were referred to ironically as 'Hitler's Gift' to the Western allies. Before Oppenheimer undertook the first bomb test, some of his leading scientists – most notably the Hungarian-Jewish Edward Teller – raised the possibility that a nuclear explosion might ignite the atmosphere and incinerate all life on earth. Oppenheimer assigned the head of his theoretical physics department, the German-Jewish Hans Bethe, to calculate the likelihood of this taking place.

Although the secret report he and Teller eventually produced claimed that such a conflagration was not possible, they did nonetheless feel constrained to add:

> However, the complexity of the argument and the absence of satisfactory experimental foundations makes further work on the subject highly desirable.

The detonation of the first atomic bomb went ahead none-theless.

The same question arose again in 1952 prior to the detonation of the first hydrogen bomb, this time masterminded by Teller himself. Once again, after meticulous calculations it was concluded that the possibility of atmospheric ignition was negligible. The first hydrogen bomb was duly tested. It immediately became apparent that not all the meticulous calculations concerning this bomb had been correct – or even approximately correct. The detonation itself proved to be *two and a half times* more powerful than the maths had predicted.

Within a few years, struggle between the two great empires competing for global domination, the United States and the Soviet Union, had achieved *reductio ad absurdum*: both had accumulated nuclear arsenals capable of destroying the world several times over. In 1962 their rivalry came to a head with the Cuban Missile Crisis. This was essentially an eyeball to eyeball confrontation between the USA and the USSR, where the Soviets 'blinked first' and Armageddon was narrowly averted. According to nuclear historian Alex Wellerstein, writing several decades later, the Cuban Crisis was 'even more dangerous than most people realised at the time, and more dangerous than most people know now.'

This was but one of several 'near-accidents' in which one of the two great modern empires might have destroyed the world rather than accept defeat. Perhaps the best-documented incident concerns 'the man who saved the world'. On 6 September 1983 Lieutenant-Colonel Stanislav Petrov was the duty officer in charge of the Serpukhov-15 nuclear early warning bunker outside Moscow. Just after midnight, one of his computers relayed information from a Soviet satellite that had detected an inbound American intercontinental ballistic missile.

In keeping with the 'deterrent' policy of mutually assured destruction (MAD), adopted by both the USA and the USSR at the time, Petrov should immediately have launched a massive simultaneous nuclear counter-attack. Instead, he decided that the computer reading must be an error and disobeyed his orders, on the grounds that if the US were to launch a first-strike attack against the Soviet Union, it would obviously involve more than one single missile. Soon, his computers indicated four more incoming missiles. Although Petrov had no means of verifying his hunch, he once again decided that these too were the result of a computer error, simply a remarkable coincidence. Once again, he desisted from launching a counter-attack.

According to later reports on this incident:

> It was subsequently determined that the false alarms were caused by a rare alignment of sunlight on high-altitude clouds and the satellites' . . . orbits, an error later corrected by cross-referencing a geostationary satellite.

Each of these three tales illuminates aspects in the creation of empire: the sense of adventure, the administration involved, as well as the dogged pursuit and exercise of sheer power. And as we have seen, such achievements frequently incorporate elements of their own self-destruction – to say nothing of any ensuing imaginative distortion of the facts concerned. The multiplicity of synchronised organisation that goes into the creation and function of a great empire is certainly humanity's most complex achievement, responsible for much of our formative historical evolution. Yet ironically, the annals of empire are frequently more concerned with ethos than historical record. Our impression of empire, whether informed or jingoistic, remains ambiguous to this day – as reflected in the following two brief images from modern culture.

In Franz Kafka's short story, *In The Penal Colony*, a colonial officer shows a visitor the ingenious machine which has been developed by his master. Anyone found guilty of an offence is strapped into the machine, which then slowly and excruciatingly inscribes upon his body the law that he has broken, torturing him to death in the process. The colonial officer is so besotted with this machine that he insists upon personally demonstrating it to his visitor. Having set the machine to inscribe the words 'Be Just', he places himself inside it. Unfortunately, the machine has fallen into disrepair, so that instead of carrying out its intricate operation it goes out of control and begins to mutilate the officer, inflicting upon him an excruciating death. It is not difficult to interpret this enigmatic imperial image in all manner of ways, few of them optimistic.

The second image is equally paradoxical, if a little less excruciating. This comes from the film, *Monty Python's Life of Brian*. In one scene, the leader of the People's Front of Judea, played by John Cleese, holds a clandestine meeting where he delivers a speech urging the party faithful to throw off the yoke of the Roman Empire. He ends by demanding rhetorically: 'What have the Romans ever done for us?' One by one the party members come up with unsolicited suggestions, until eventually their leader is forced to exclaim exasperatedly:

All right . . . all right . . . but apart from better sanitation and medicine and education and irrigation and public health and roads and a freshwater system and baths and public order . . . what *have* the Romans done for *us*?

These three tales of empire, and the ensuing two images, may be viewed as paradigms of the wider generality of empire itself and how we have come to regard it.

All of which brings us to the thorny topic of what precisely constitutes an empire? What is its definition? Does this remain the same throughout world history? And indeed, what is the effect on world history of such entities? The *Oxford English Dictionary* definition of an empire is:

> An extensive territory (*esp.* an aggregate of many separate states) under the sway of an emperor or supreme ruler; also an aggregate of separate territories ruled over by a sovereign state.

Here we have but a basic framework. Inevitably, over the centuries this will take on different guises – not all of which will involve what we would regard as progressive elements of evolution.

As indicated earlier, a description of empire must be deemed to subsume such elements as the spirit of adventure, administration, and power – initially in the form of war. Indeed, war and consequent subjugation of alien people would seem to be the formative impulse from which empire develops. 'Civilising' aspects frequently, but not invariably, follow. It seems no accident that civilisation (in its Western form) progressed across the globe more rapidly than ever before during the century which saw the first two world wars, followed by the threat of a third.

On the other hand, since the last decades of that century, and well into this one, the world has seen no major wars on that previous scale, while progress, especially in the form of the IT revolution and all that entails, has transformed the world as never before. Bearing in mind such multifarious aspects of empire, we can now begin to trace the history of the world as it is reflected in ten supreme examples of this phenomenon.

I

The Akkadian Empire

Around 5,000 years ago, settled agricultural communities of
the late Bronze Age began to coalesce into recognisable,
socially organised civilisations in three distinct regions of the
globe. The earliest of these emerged prior to 3000 BC in
the Fertile Crescent, which stretches in a hoop from Upper
Egypt along the Eastern Mediterranean coast, and down the
Tigris-Euphrates valley to the Persian Gulf. Similar developments would occur around 2500 BC in the Indus Valley
(loosely modern Pakistan) and half a millennium later along
the Yellow River in China. Central to all these regions are
great rivers, which irrigate the land and are prone to flooding.
Herodotus, 'the father of history', writing in the fifth century
BC, offers one of the earliest descriptions:

> During the flooding of the Nile only the towns are visible,
> rising above the surface of the water like the scattered
> islands of the Aegean Sea. While the inundation continues,
> boats no longer keep to the channels and rivers, but sail
> across the fields and plains.

In distant history, such an inundation had evidently become
a catastrophic deluge, carrying away all in its path. Thus

it comes as little surprise that the early mythology of each
of these separate civilisations speaks of a great flood which
God caused to cover the earth, with only a chosen few
surviving. In the biblical version, it is Noah and his family
who survive, along with their ark, which contained 'two
and two of all flesh' including 'every beast . . . and all the
cattle . . . every creeping thing that creepeth upon the earth
. . . and every fowl [and] every bird.' When the Flood
subsided, Noah's ark is said to have run aground on Mt
Ararat, which is located in the far east of modern Turkey,
close to the borders with Armenia and Iran, at the very
upper reaches of the Euphrates river basin.

At the opposite ends of the Fertile Crescent, in Egypt
and in Mesopotamia (loosely modern Iraq), two distinct
civilisations began to develop. In Egypt, the so-called Old
Kingdom began in 2686 BC with the unification of the
Upper and Lower Kingdoms. Perhaps half a millennium
prior to this, the Sumerian civilisation attained maturity in
the fertile region between the Tigris and Euphrates rivers,
which during this period flowed separately into the Persian
Gulf.[1] Technological innovations which took place within
the Fertile Crescent include the development of agriculture
and the introduction of irrigation, as well as the invention
of glass-making and the wheel.

Writing was invented by the Sumerians. Originally this
consisted of round marks made in damp clay, which was
then baked to become a permanent record – probably
numbering cattle, containers of wheat and so forth. With

---

1 Owing to silting and the Tigris-Euprates delta, the north-western
coast of the Persian Gulf has now moved some 100 miles south-east
of its location in ancient times.

the introduction of a wedge-shaped reed as a marker, these impresses evolved into cuneiform writing, with distinct characters, capable of conveying things and later the language itself. Sumerian, as spoken in southern Mesopotamia, is classified as a 'language isolate'; in other words, it appears to be original, and not descended from any prior language – except perhaps an early verbal Paleolithic pidgin. The Sumerians inhabited independent city states, whose populations probably extended to around 20–30,000 inhabitants each. The territorial boundaries of these states were marked out by canals and boundary stones. In the view of most authorities, the Sumerians may have constituted a civilisation, but they were not an empire. Yet it was out of this innovative civilisation that the Akkadian Empire (2334–2154 BC)would grow.

One of the earliest references to Akkad is in the Book of Genesis, the first book of the Bible. This records that Nimrod, the great grandson of Noah, founded a kingdom which included Babel and 'Accad'. According to myth, Nimrod was responsible for building the Tower of Babel, a structure intended to be so high that it would reach heaven. This so angered God that he caused its builders to speak different languages, thus confounding their efforts, and dividing humanity into different language groups. Some myths also identify Nimrod with Gilgamesh, hero of the eponymous Epic, the oldest great work of literature known to us. From this, it can be seen that Nimrod is probably a mythical character, containing elements of several ancient heroes whose identity became blurred in prehistory.

The first historically certain ruler of the Akkadian Empire was Sargon, who was born around the middle of the twenty-third century BC. Though we do not know the actual birth-name of this individual: Sargon simply means 'the true king'. Even details of Sargon's life and reign remain disputed amongst scholars, necessitating choice, which once again leaves any historian open to the charge of valuing ethos over accumulated fact, incorporating often contradictory evidence.

Sargon's legendary description of his infancy has familiar overtones:

> My mother was a changeling [a child substituted by fairies for a human child], my father I knew not . . . She set me in a basket of rushes, with bitumen sealing my lid. She cast me into the river which rose not over me . . .

In this there are unmistakable echoes of the infant Moses, the Hindu god Krishna, and Oedipus, as well as the Messiah. This would appear to be some kind of archetypal myth, a requisite for such early proto- or quasi-divine figures. Much like Moses almost a millennium later, Sargon was found, adopted and thrived in his new home, the kingdom of Kish, part of the original Sumerian civilisation. Sargon rose to the important post of maintaining the irrigation of the kingdom's canals, in charge of a large band of labourers. These labourers were probably reserve militia, skilled in the use of weapons. At any rate, Sargon gained their loyalty, and they aided him in overthrowing the King of Kish, Ur-Zababa, around 2354 BC.

Soon after seizing power, Sargon succeeded in conquering a number of neighbouring Sumerian cities, including Ur, Uruk, and possibly Babylon. After every victory he 'tore down the city walls' and the city was incorporated into the

Akkadian Empire. Sargon is said to have founded the capital Akkad (Accad, Aggade). According to one source, he 'dug up the soil of the pit of Babylon, and made a counterpart of Babylon next to Agade.' Here Sargon built his palace, set up his administration and barracks for his army. He established a temple to Ishtar (Akkadian name for the Sumerian goddess of fertility and war) and Zababa (the warrior god of Kish). Sadly, Akkad has yet to be discovered, and remains 'the only royal city of ancient Iraq whose location remains unknown.' This precludes any direct archaeological evidence, limiting our knowledge to the likes of Babylonian tablets and texts, often made many centuries later.

Sargon's ambitions soon grew, and he would launch a number of campaigns – with the declared intention of extending his empire across the entire known world, as it was to him. This included the whole of the Fertile Crescent, no less. He did not ultimately succeed in this, but the extent of his conquests and military expeditions remains impressive all the same. The later Babylonian texts, known as the 'Sargon Epos', speak of him seeking the advice of his subordinate commanders before launching his ambitious campaigns. This suggests the commander of a well-run military machine, rather than a despotic ruler, or the megalomania implied by his territorial aims. Not surprisingly his feats entered later legend:

[Sargon] had neither rival nor equal. His splendor, over the lands it diffused. He crossed the sea in the east. In the eleventh year he conquered the western land to its farthest point. He brought it under one authority. He set up his statues there and ferried the west's booty across on barges.

He stationed his court officials at intervals of five double hours and ruled in unity the tribes of the lands. He marched to Kazallu and turned Kazallu into a ruin heap, so that there was not even a perch for a bird left.

Kazallu seems to have been one of Sargon's earliest conquests, as it was probably located east of the Euphrates near Babylon. The ultimate extent of Sargon's conquests remains impressive. His military exploits certainly took him as far as the eastern shores of the Mediterranean 'up to the cedar forest and the silver mountain'. This is seen as a reference to the Ammanus and Taurus ranges, which stretch along the border of Anatolia (modern Turkey). Some legends suggest that he marched beyond this into Anatolia itself. This makes sense, as hostile tribes occupied the passes through these mountains, thus controlling the Akkadian trade routes to Anatolia, Armenia and Azerbaijan from which they received their supplies of tin, copper and silver.

The presence of such tribes may also account for why Sargon launched his southern military expeditions, which would have secured trade routes to these same metals in south-east Persia and Oman. This, or a further campaign into eastern territory, would also have protected access to the lapis lazuli which originated in north-east Afghanistan. This semi-precious stone, whose intense blue colour was much valued, could be polished for use in beads, amulets and inlays for statuettes. The extent of Sargon's southern military expeditions is known in more detail. He is said to have 'washed his weapons in the sea', i.e. the Persian Gulf.[2]

---

2 In time, this became a ritual of Akkadian rulers, marking the successful end of a campaign or war.

Sargon's southern conquests extended along the north-eastern shores of the Persian Gulf as far as the Straits of Hormuz. Records of another expedition have him extending his empire along the south-western shores of the Gulf as far as Dilmun (modern Bahrain) and Magan (Oman). Such feats may seem extraordinary, but they remain plausible. Sargon is said to have maintained a standing army-cum-court of 5,400 men, 'who ate bread daily before him'. Later texts speak of him setting sail across the Sea of the West (the Mediterranean) and reaching Keftiu, or Caphtor as it is called in the Bible. This is usually taken to be Cyprus, or possibly even Crete. Such was Sargon's empire that he is said to have declared: 'Now, any king who wants to call himself my equal, wherever I went, let him go!'

As we shall see, the leaders (and citizens) of most consequent great empires will harbour similar grandiose sentiments, which resonate through the millennia, mocking, and yet later mocked by, those who follow. This paradox is perhaps best illustrated by Shelley's poem on 'Ozymandias, king of kings', who boasted, 'Look on my works, ye mighty, and despair.' Yet all that now remained of these works was a vast broken statue and its half buried, shattered stone head, beyond which 'boundless and bare the lone and level sands stretch far away'. Sargon was the first Ozymandias.[3] And the lesson has yet to be learned, even today. From the Roman emperors to Napoleon, Hitler and beyond, dreams of imperial greatness remain rooted in a present which extends into perpetuity.

---

3 In fact, Shelley based his poem upon the pharaoh Ramesses II, who would rule in Ancient Egypt a millennium or so later.

Babylonian copies of inscriptions that are known to date
from the early Akkadian era claim that Sargon ruled over
his empire for fifty-five years (*c.*2334–2279 BC). His extension of territory certainly aimed at more than mere conquest
and devastation, as in the case of Kazallu. In many cities
he appears to have spared the indigenous population,
replacing the local government with Akkadian administrators. Likewise, the previous ruler would be executed and
a trusted deputy installed in his place. With devastated
cities such as Kazallu, the remnant population would either
be put to the sword, or marched off in captivity to become
slaves, in much the same manner as the Bible describes
the Israelites being led into captivity in Babylon over one
and a half millennia later.

In Sargon's early conquests of Sumerian cities, he is said
to have placed his daughter Enheduana as high-priestess
of the moon god Inanna in Ur, and extended her role to
high-priestess of the god of heaven, An, at nearby Uruk.
Enheduana was evidently well suited for such roles, and
she is known to have written a number of hymns to these
Sumerian gods, which played a significant role in winning
over the local population to her father's rule. As such, she
stakes a remarkable claim:

> Sargon's daughter made herself the first identifiable author
> in history, and the first to express a personal relationship
> between herself and her god.

These are two highly significant steps in our social indi-
viduation. Previously worshippers had grovelled in fear
before their gods. Enheduana establishes herself as more
than a mere priest. She wishes to be taken as a person, an

interlocutor with the gods. She speaks to them personally, telling them what is happening in their cities. When a certain Lugal-Ane leads a rebellion at Ur, she asks Inanna to pass on a message to An, asking him to right these wrongs and come to her aid:

> Wise and sage lady of all foreign lands,
> Life-force of the teeming people:
> I will recite your holy song! . . .
> Lugal-Ane has altered everything,
> He has removed An from E-Ana temple . . .
> He stood there in triumph and drove me out of the
> temple.
> He made me fly like a swallow from the window;
> My life-strength is exhausted . . .
> My honeyed mouth became scummed.
> Tell An about Lugal-Ane and my fate!
> May An undo it for me!

Note how Inanna, initially goddess of the city of Ur, is addressed as 'lady of all foreign lands', suggesting that her rule now extends over all her father's conquests. The significance of this will become apparent later. At any rate, Enheduana's prayers are answered, the rebellion is overcome, and she is reinstated, whereupon she addresses a profuse hymn of praise to Inanna: 'My lady beloved of An . . .'

However, such a rebellion was not an isolated incident. As Sargon grew older, his grip on his empire was thought to be faltering. According to a late Babylonian chronicle: 'In his old age all the lands revolted against him, and they besieged him in Agade.' But Sargon was still prepared to rouse himself against 'any king who wants to call himself my equal'. From his besieged capital he launched a furious counter-attack: 'he went forth to battle and defeated them; he knocked them over and destroyed their vast army'. Later, the nomadic hill tribes of upper Mesopotamia rose against him, and 'in their might attacked, but they submitted to his arms, and Sargon settled their habitations, and smote them grievously'.

As we shall see, this tendency to revolt in the outer regions of the Akkadian Empire would become a regular feature in the later years of a ruler's life. Sargon was succeeded by his son Rimush, whose accession was greeted by a further revolt amongst the Sumerians and further afield in Persia. Although Rimush forcefully subdued these uprisings, he appears to have been a weak and unpopular character. Ultimately, he even forfeited the loyalty of his own courtiers. In 2270 BC, after nine years of rule, 'his servants killed him with their tablets.' As the twentieth-century French historian, Georges Roux, wryly comments, this 'is proof that the written word was already a deadly weapon'.

Ramish's successor to the throne was Manishtushu, whose name means 'Who is with him?' Roux suggests that this indicates he was Ramish's twin brother. He too appears to have appointed his daughter as a high-priestess, which would suggest that this was becoming customary. The main event of Manishtushu's reign was a great campaign he led south to the Persian Gulf:

Manishtushu, King of Kish . . . crossed the Lower Sea [Gulf] in ships. The kings of the cities on either side of the sea, thirty-two of them assembled for battle. He defeated

them and subjugated their cities; he overthrew their lords
and seized the whole country as far as the silver mines.
The mountains beyond the Lower Sea – their stones he
took away, and he made his statue . . .

Access to the trade routes in the south was once again
open, giving access to metals and lapis lazuli. This was just
as well, for by now the northern territories of the empire
had slipped from Akkadian grasp, their lands overrun by
hostile neighbours.

After a fourteen-year rule, Manishtushu would be
succeeded by his son, Narâm-Sin, whose name translates
as 'Beloved of [the people of] Sin'. He would prove to be
a great ruler, in the mould of his grandfather; his thirty-
six-year reign (2254–2218 BC) inspiring many legends of
his greatness. Having inherited the title 'King of Agade',
Narâm-Sin would later add 'King of the Four Regions (of
the World)', eventually ascending to 'King of the Universe',
with his written name preceded by the star, ideogram
meaning 'god', which in Sumerian reads as *dingir*, and in
Akkadian as *ilu*.

This brings us to the difficult question of language.
Although both the Akkadians and the Sumerians were
Semitic peoples, they spoke distinctly different languages.
It was Sargon who introduced Akkadian as the official
language of government administration and imperial trade.
Akkadian is the first Semitic language of which we have
written evidence, and its main dialects appear to have been
Babylonian and Assyrian. However, the original Sumerian
remained the ceremonial and religious language. This was
possibly because the Akkadians tended to adopt the gods
of conquered territories, yet at the same time appointing

female members of the royal family as their high-priestesses to ensure religious loyalty.

This transformation of the Akkadian language meant that it would become the spoken language throughout the empire. On the other hand, some scholars insist that Sumerian was retained and that the Akkadian Empire saw 'widespread bilingualism'. As we have seen, Sumerian was a 'language isolate', whereas Akkadian was an East Semitic language – one of six groups in the Semitic language as a whole, which itself spread over the Levant, the Middle East, the Arabian peninsula and the Abyssinian region.

The general use of Akkadian and East Semitic through the Akkadian Empire led to 'stylised borrowing on a substantial scale, to syntactic, morphological and phonological convergence'. Indeed, Akkadian would remain the lingua franca throughout the region until a millennium later, whence came the rise of Aramaic (the language spoken by Christ). Ironically, both Akkadian and East Semitic eventually became extinct, whereas the Semitic languages as a whole would evolve into widespread use in such varied languages as Phoenician, the Punic language of Carthage, as well as Arabic, Amharic (Ethiopian) and Hebrew.[4]

The imperial administration was funded by taxes on vassal city states, which were also required to maintain Akkadian garrisons. Domination was further maintained by the royal monopoly on foreign trade, as well as the awarding of estates in conquered territory to what is best

---

4 Spoken Ancient Hebrew fell into disuse around AD 300, remaining only in written Biblical and religious usage. It was revived in its modern form in the early twentieth century by the Russian-born scholar Eliezer Ben Yehuda, and became the official language of the state of Israel.

described as Akkadian aristocracy. These were mostly former military commanders and trusted administrators, who would also be rewarded with slaves originating from other conquered cities. This had the added advantage of dispersing members of any potential clique who might attempt to overthrow their supreme ruler.

The power of the imperial ruler was further reinforced by his elevation to divine status. This had the effect of enhancing his personal charisma. It is difficult to over-stress this element of 'leadership-charisma', which would be a recurrent feature of empires. Emperors would be descended from the divine members of their family, thus assuming deity. Mere mortals who trembled in the emperor-god's presence could never escape his wrath, even in the after-life.

One of the great early Akkadian inventions was Sargon's calendar, which was used throughout the empire. Sargon would name each year after an important event which had taken place during the previous year, and this became a standard tradition:

> *The year when Sargon went to Simurrum,*
> *The year when Naram-Sin* [sic] *conquered . . . and felled*
>   *cedars on Mount Lebanon.*

Thus all city records were synchronised with those of Akkad. Before this, each city worked according to its own calendar – though in some cases religious events would coincide, owing to their dates coinciding with astronomical events, such as the equinox. Apart from its practical value, Sargon's calendar was the most obvious symbol of a more pervasive imperial assimilation. Prior to conquest, each

Sumerian city had used its own system of weights and measures, as well as distances. Under Sargon and subsequent rulers, all such measurements became standardised throughout Mesopotamia.[5] This further cemented Akkadian rule, helping to establish a common way of life amongst the subject people. Furthermore, such was the success of this system that these were 'units which would remain standard for over one thousand years.'

Towards the end of Narâm-Sin's thirty-six-year reign, he became 'bewildered, confused, sunk in gloom, sorrowful, exhausted'. The usual end-of-reign uprisings appear to have taken place in the outer provinces, most notably amongst the powerful Lullubi in Persia. Most inscriptions record that Narâm-Sin was victorious in these struggles, but this may include an element of rose-tinted hindsight. Other (admittedly incomplete) inscriptions speak of defeats, with Narâm-Sin only able to make a successful last stand at Agade. Either way, there is no denying that Narâm-Sin was 'the last great monarch of the Akkadian dynasty'. His first notable victory over the Lullubi is commemorated in a fine rock sculpture, which can still be seen near a mountain-top in modern Iran at Darband-i Gawr (Pass of the Pagan).

More pertinently, he is also depicted in a superb victory stele, which was discovered at Susa, north of the Persian Gulf. This has deservedly been characterised as 'a masterpiece of Mesopotamian sculpture'. Besides its realistic depiction in relief of surprisingly lifelike human figures, it has a number of significant features. For instance,

---

5 Mesopotamia is in fact the later Greek word for this region, meaning 'the land between between two rivers', i.e. the Tigris and the Euphrates.

Narâm-Sin is depicted as being almost twice as tall as the other human figures beneath him, and he is wearing a two-horned helmet, a sign of his divinity. (Later, this would become the sign of a minor deity; as a major deity, his helmet would sprout four horns.)[6]

Such regular end-of-reign uprisings allow us to make certain deductions. As the twentieth-century author Paul Kriwaczek pointed out:

> Empires based solely on power and domination, while allowing their subjects to do as they will, can last for centuries. Those that try to control the everyday lives of their people are much harder to sustain.

Such considerations certainly help account for the brevity of this first empire, which lasted for less than two centuries.[7] The Akkadian imposition of alien gods upon their conquered cities would seem to have been but the outward manifestation of a more heavy-handed communal control. Even so, other factors must certainly have contributed. For a start, the sheer novelty of this highly complex human-social creation must certainly have made it difficult to sustain. Obvious though it may seem, one should always bear in mind the sheer difficulty presented by the fact that the Akkadians had no blueprint for what they were doing. They were obliged to make up the rules as they went along.

---

6 Narâm-Sin's stele can be seen at the Louvre in Paris.

7 To put this into context: such a period constitutes around half the length of the British Empire, and is the equivalent of the entire British Empire at its zenith.

Following the death of Narâm-Sin in 2218 BC, he was succeeded by his son, Shar-kali-sharri ('King of All Kings'), who would rule for the next twenty-five years. Shar-kali-sharri appears to have presided over a period of almost continuous provincial revolts, even one by the governor of Elam, who had been appointed by his father. In 2193 BC, Shar-kali-sharri would be murdered in a palace revolt, whereupon the empire descended into anarchy. The Sumerian King List, which was compiled around 2100 BC, evocatively says of this period: 'Who was king? Who was not king?'

Excavations carried out at the end of the twentieth century indicate that from *c*.2220–2000 BC the entire Eastern Mediterranean region was subject to a severe climate change, bringing with it droughts and famine. During this period, fertile regions in Sinai became deserts, and archaeological evidence indicates that 'nearly all Palestinian . . . towns and villages were destroyed around 2200 BC and lay abandoned for about two centuries.' Some posit a sensational explanation for this climate change: 'Aerial photographs of southern Iraq revealed a two-mile-wide circular depression with the classic hallmarks of a meteor crater.' This would possibly explain recent archaeological evidence that on some sites there was 'construction seemingly going well when, apparently overnight, all work suddenly stopped.'

Either way, this change marked the end of the Akkadian Empire, regarded by many as 'The First World Empire'.

However, not all concur with this assessment. The twentieth-century Italian scholar, Mario Liverani, vehemently insists: 'In no case is the Akkad empire an absolute novelty [. . .] "Akkad the first empire" is therefore subject to criticism not only as for the adjective "first" but especially as for the noun "empire".' Liverani argues that earlier the Sumerians developed 'proto-imperial states', adding somewhat anomalously that the term 'empire' with regard to the Akkadians is 'simplistic'.

This argument is convincingly countered by Kriwaczek, who points out a fundamental transformation that came about with this 'first empire': 'Up until now, civilisation based itself on the belief that humanity was created by the gods for their own purposes . . . Each city was the creation and home of a particular god.' With the conquests of Sargon, all this changed. This was how Inanna, goddess of the city of Ur, came to be addressed by Sargon's daughter Enheduana as 'lady of all foreign lands'. The gods and goddesses of the rulers would become the supreme gods and goddesses of the entire Akkadian Empire.

The Akkadian world witnessed the proliferation, if not always the origin, of many features of early civilisation. Sophisticated realistic sculptures were carved in relief on stone stele, or gouged in relief into cylinders, which, when rolled, left an impression in clay. Similarly, silver gathered from mines at the outposts of the empire was melted into ingots. These were then stamped with a name (the seal of approval) and weight; they were thus used for trade: a proto-form of money, guaranteed by the world's first bankers.

The Akkadians also built the first ziggurats: stepped asymmetrical flat-topped pyramidal structures with temples at their summit. The very word ziggurat is an anglicised form of the original Akkadian 'ziqquratu', and in time one of the greatest of these would be a 300-foot-high Babylonian ziggurat named Etemenanki. Although this huge structure is now reduced to nothing but rubble, its name translates as 'home of the platform between heaven and earth', confirming that these were the edifices that gave rise to the legend of the Tower of Babel. Although no temples have yet been found at the summit of any extant ziggurats, we know of their existence.

The Ziggurat of Ur, which rises to 100 feet. Some such structures are known to have been three times this size.

Herodotus describes the furnishing of the shrine on top of the ziggurat at Babylon and says it contained a great golden couch, on which a woman spent the night alone. The god Marduk was also said to come and sleep in his shrine. Thus, the son of god was the issue of a god and a human woman, an early example of the story that would persist through Zeus in the Greek myths into the Christian era.

Speculations on the precise origins of the ziggurats

are equally intriguing. Some claim that they represent a sacred mountain, a folk-memory from the original Sumerian homeland, which according to some sources was 'the mountains of the north-east'. This suggests the Zagros Mountains, which occupy western Persia and border the Fertile Crescent. A similarly plausible suggestion, which in no way contradicts the mountain myth, claims these ziggurats were raised as protection for the temples against the seasonal floods, some of which could be extreme.

As their architecture grew, there is no doubt that they were intended to become increasingly awesome and forbidding to the common people gathered below. The complicated sets of staircases worked into their design would have made them easy to defend against intruders, at the same time preventing any secular spies from discovering the secrets of the temple ceremonies and initiation rituals. Once again, echoes of such practices have come down to us in the Eleusinian Mysteries of the Ancient Greeks, later ritual sacrifices of many kinds, and remnants can even be detected in the high altars of Christian churches.

Only priests were permitted to ascend to the top of ziggurats, and one of their duties was to observe the movements of the stars in the night heavens. Here astronomy was certainly entwined with astrology: yet the astronomical understanding of the movements of the planets developed by these priests would later enable the Babylonians accurately to predict eclipses of the sun many centuries into the future. These used advanced geometric techniques that would not be rediscovered in Europe until the fourteenth century AD.

Sequence

What originated with the Akkadians would be developed
by the Babylonians, who gave the world further distinctive features of early civilisation and empire. Not least
of these was the Code of Hammurabi, the world's earliest
comprehensive code of laws. This was inscribed in
Akkadian on a seven-foot-high stele dating from around
1754 BC during the reign of the Babylonian king
Hammurabi. It contains 282 laws, covering aspects of
civil life ranging from slander to theft and divorce, as
well as most famously the legal principle paraphrased as
'an eye for an eye . . .'

Meanwhile some 700 miles or so to the west of Babylon,
a parallel empire was developing in the form of Ancient
Egypt. Here too a civilisation evolved its own similar, yet
distinctive hallmarks, such as pyramids, the successive rule
of pharaonic god-kings, and hieroglyphic writing, in this
case on papyrus. The Egyptians also developed their own
more down-to-earth, but equally impressive, form of mathematics. Each year the Nile flood would recede, leaving
bare mudflats, which would have to be divided into plots
of land precisely commensurate with those occupied prior
to the rising flood. This led to a mathematics involving
immensely complicated algebraic fractions (whereas the
Babylonian mathematics had more of a tendency towards
abstract geometric precision).

H.G. Wells, writing a century ago, would claim of these
empires:

> We know that life for prosperous and influential people in
> such cities as Babylon and the Egyptian Thebes, was already

almost as refined and as luxurious as that of comfortable and prosperous people today.

This may well be, yet it is always worth bearing in mind P.J. O'Rourke's advice: 'When you are thinking of the good old days, think one word: Dentistry.' Quite aside from this painful art, it is worth considering another significant dental fact. The teeth of Ancient Egyptian mummies (i.e. the fortunate few described above) are invariably flat. This was initially ascribed to evolutionary reasons. It is now known that they were ground down by the amount of desert sand and grit that could not be prevented from entering prepared food. And to dental hardships one could add life expectancy, virulent disfiguring diseases, the vice-like conformity required by such societies . . . sufficient imagination can always add to this list.

Such strictures will apply, in more or less a degree, to all empires great and small, before and after Ancient Egypt. It is the ethos that can be rosy, instructive, inspirational, and so forth – seldom the nitty-teeth-gritty facts. But this should not be a cause for pessimism. History scrutinises the past, and seeks to learn from it: it does not seek to live in it.

Egyptian influences would spread to Crete, with Babylonian influences dispersing through Anatolia and Persia, while the Phoenicians transported such ideas throughout the Mediterranean. Amongst the Greek-speaking city states that occupied the islands and coasts of the Aegean, this would produce a transformation. Uniquely, Ancient Greek civilisation was fragmented, while its learning was divorced from religion. Liberated from an oppressive all-embracing imperial and religious hierarchy, individualistic thought blossomed, giving birth to what we now see as Western civilisation.

Object	Hebrew	Egyptian	Phoenician	Early Greek	Roman
Ox head	Aleph	𐤀	⟨	Λ	A
House plan	Beth	☐	𝄐	⊿	B
Joy	He	ⵤ	⋺	⋺	E
Hand	Kaf	⬭	Ψ	⪤	K
Water	Mem	∿∿	⋏	⋏	M
Snake	Nun	⟋	⟙	⟙	N
Eye	Ayin	⬮	O	o	O
Mouth	Pe	⬯	⟑	⟑	P
Teeth	Shin	⟶	W	⟨	S

Examples of evolving alphabet

Philosophy, democracy, citizens' rights, the perfection of realistic sculpture, architecture, science, tragedy, comedy even, the list goes on . . . such creative individual freedom (for all but women and slaves) would become a template for Western civilisation. Once this strain of mentality had become established, it would never quite be eliminated from Western human evolution. Over the following two and a half millennia, it would survive tyranny, state terror, empires, barbarism, and even centuries of intellectual stagnation. However, from the outset, this mental trait would prove ineffective in combatting sheer physical power. For all its glories, the Greek world would quickly succumb to the military might of the expanding Roman Empire.

Despite such radical developments, there was no clear-cut break with earlier empires. This is perhaps most significantly illustrated by an unmistakable thread of continuity in the evolution of alphabetical writing, which gradually replaced cuneiform scripts such as Akkadian and Babylonian.

2

The Roman Empire

The founding legend of Rome is replete with familiar echoes. A vestal virgin named Rhea Silvia, one of the priestesses who tended the sacred flame, was seduced by Mars, the god of war. When she gave birth to twins, named Romulus and Remus, these were placed in a reed basket, which floated away down the River Tiber. The twins were rescued by a she-wolf, who suckled them. Later Romulus would slay Remus (just as the biblical Cain had slain Abel), and in 753 BC he would found the city named after him on the Palatine Hill overlooking the Tiber.

To encourage the growth of this new settlement, its king Romulus welcomed colonists, giving refuge to fugitives and slaves. Most of these colonists were young men, so Romulus invited the nearby Sabines to a festival, where the Romans abducted and raped the young Sabine women. Consequently, the Romans found themselves plunged into a series of wars against neighbouring tribes in order to ensure their continuing existence. To assist him in his rule, Romulus appointed a hundred old men. The Latin for old man is 'senex', and this group became known as the Senate, an institution that would survive throughout the entire era of the Roman Empire.

As we shall see, these early legends contain in embryo an

uncanny resemblance to many of the fundamental elements that would characterise the Roman Empire. In particular, ruthlessness and aggression. Militarism would be central to Rome's social structure – enabling it first to survive, and then to thrive. Of all the empires we shall describe, it is the Roman which casts the longest shadow over ensuing history. Indeed, some elements would even persist into that very perpetuity dreamt of by all empires. To this day, the traditional depiction of the she-wolf suckling the infants Romulus and Remus remains an iconic image in the city of Rome. And over a millennium and a half after the fall of Ancient Rome, its proud acronym SPQR (*Senatus Populusque Romanus*: 'The Senate and People of Rome') remains the official emblem of the municipality, visible on everything from manhole covers to pavement refuse bins.

A modern Roman manhole cover.

Of course, the city – which would spread from the Palatine Hill to the traditional seven hills of Rome – is also filled with monuments to its ancient imperial past: ruins, complete sites, roads, aqueducts and so forth. Much the same is true throughout the former territory of the empire, which in a recurrent theme its poet Virgil named the 'Empire without limit'. Remnants stretch across Europe and beyond, from Hadrian's Wall near the border of Scotland to the Hadrian's Arch on the fringes of the Arabian Desert (in modern-day Jordan). And most pervasive of all, the Latin language, which remains more or less recognisable in the many European languages that evolved from the original mother tongue – such as Italian, Spanish, French, Romanian, and a considerable part of English. So many words in all these languages would be easily discernible to any educated Ancient Roman.

Then there are the legal systems, weights and measures, municipal baths even, architecture – to name but a few formative influences. For example, Peter Charles L'Enfant, the French military engineer who originally designed Washington DC in the early 1790s, intended its government buildings to resemble a neo-classical Rome.

From the early years, the people of Rome and its senators adopted a constitution, consisting of an unwritten set of principles, mainly established through precedent. At least in theory, the king was appointed by the senate. And the constitution contained many elements that remain the *sine qua non* of national constitutions to this day, i.e. the notion of checks and balances, to ensure that no power group can gain undue influence.[8] Also, the separation of powers, such as the independence of government and justice, religion

---

8 The italic phrase meaning 'without which not' (essential) and the abbreviation 'i.e.' for *id est* ('that is'), indicate how much unadulterated Latin remains in our language to this day.

and state, and so forth. And, perhaps most important of all, the notion of impeachment, by which the legislature could lay formal charge against its leader.

The king was accompanied by an armed guard of lictors, each bearing the fasces, a bundle of rods strapped around an axe. This symbol of power has reverberated through the ages – appearing on the back of the pre-Second World War US dime, as well as behind the podium in the US House of Representatives. It also gave its name to the modern term fascism.

During the initial Kingdom of Rome period (753–476 BC) the city gradually overcame the powerful Etruscan civilisation, which occupied the swathe of territory north of Rome, running through Tuscany and beyond, and to the south as far as modern Naples. When the seventh king, Tarquinius Superbus (Tarquin the Proud), attempted to institute a hereditary monarchy, the kings were overthrown and the senate established a republic (from *res publica*: the 'public thing'). This was ruled by the senate, now expanded to several hundred patricians (upper class families), which appointed two consuls, who held office for a year each. The republic also included an assembly of tribunes, elected by the plebeians (the common people). This lower house could propose laws to be voted on by the senate. Such a bi-cameral structure of government remains a recognisable feature of democracies to this day.

The consuls would often become military commanders, leading the army during times of war. As Roman power expanded through southern Italy and Sicily, it soon came up against the Phoenician people, who controlled the Mediterranean from their capital Carthage, in modern Tunisia. This would result in a war for the control of the

Mediterranean, no less – to all intents and purposes, the civilised world as they knew it. The ensuing titanic conflict against the Carthaginians would continue for over a century, and became known as the Three Punic Wars (264–146 BC). It was during the second of these wars that the Carthaginian general Hannibal led his army, including cavalry elephants, across the 'impenetrable' Alps. His surprise invasion wreaked havoc through Italy for fifteen years, at one point even besieging Rome itself.

The Romans also came under attack from the Macedonian Greeks to the east. Just over a century previously, the Macedonian leader, Alexander the Great, had conquered Anatolia, Egypt, and Persia, reaching as far as the banks of the Indus. This large, short-lived empire fell apart on his death, eventually fracturing into more than half a dozen separate states. Even so, the Macedonians remained a formidable fighting force.

Fortunately, the Romans were led by Publius Scipio, the only military strategist of the age who could match Hannibal's genius. Scipio led an invasion of North Africa, which struck at the heart of Carthage, and in 202 BC defeated Hannibal at the Battle of Zuma. Carthage sued for peace, and henceforth the victorious Roman general became known as Scipio Africanus, on account of his North African great victory, which had saved the empire and led to him becoming a consul.

During the Punic Wars, Roman power began expanding through Spain, North Africa, southern France, and perhaps most importantly of all, into Greece. At this point, Greece remained arguably a superior civilisation to the Romans, both culturally and possibly even militarily. The secret of Alexander the Great's unprecedented military success had been the Greek phalanx. Basically, this consisted of an impenetrable advancing line of soldiers with interlocked shields bearing short swords. Behind them was a similar line of soldiers with longer spears, which protruded beyond the shields of the front line. Supported by wedge-formations of cavalry, this proved an irresistible force.

Then in 197 BC, the invading Roman army came into conflict with the defending Greek army at the Battle of Cynocephalae. The Macedonian Greek forces outnumbered the Romans, but were hampered by swirling mists and the vulnerable flanks of their phalanxes. The Macedonian phalanx proved no match for the more manoeuvrable Roman legions, which were supported by cavalry, including twenty war elephants. (The Romans had learned from the Carthaginians: elephants were unstoppable, and terrified even the strongest infantry formations.)

From this point on, the Roman legions would prove all but invincible, until they reached the extremities of Gaul (France); the harrying Germanic tribes of the Rhine who disappeared into their forests and avoided fixed battles; and the Picts of northern Britannia, where according to legend the famous Ninth Legion (of 5,000 men) marched north into the mists of Caledonia, never to return, with no trace of them being discovered to this day.

The history of Ancient Rome is usually divided into three distinct eras. As we have seen, the initial Kingdom gave way to the Republic in 476 BC. It was during the four and a half centuries of the Republic that Rome expanded into an Empire. Increasingly, the republican tenor of Rome would come under threat during these years. This is best illustrated by the social situation in Rome itself. Initially, the ruling patrician families and the plebeian commoners appear to have lived in relative harmony.

This was largely due to a system of patronage, known as *clientia*, by which upper class 'patrons' looked after their lower class 'clientele'. Such patronage might typically include employment, protection, sponsorship for office and so forth – with reciprocal support for patrons. The latter indicates an important mutual aspect of this arrangement. Patrons could employ crowds of supporters, vociferously calling for political office for their paymaster. The more clientele a patron had, the more prestige he could command.

As the empire expanded, more slaves were despatched to Rome, and this arrangement of patronage came under stress. Plebeians who had been employed in menial tasks found themselves surplus to requirements. Landowners took on slaves to do their agricultural work, and important citizens even took on educated slaves as scribes. In a parallel development, the governors of provinces of the new empire became increasingly wealthy. Egypt and the Carthaginian hinterlands of Africa Vetus (Old Africa) provided increasingly large and lucrative shipments of grain.[9]

Most significant of all was the growing power that began accruing to the successful commanders, who began expanding the empire, as well as dealing with such troubles and revolts as arose within it. Amongst the legions, an aspect

---

9 Cave drawings dating from 3000 BC indicate that millet and grain were grown over much of what is now the Sahara Desert. Only gradually did the desert encroach on the arable land due in part to lack of water and the depredations of goats. Even during Roman times, North Africa remained 'the granary of the empire', producing as much as a million tons of cereals annually.

of *clientia* continued to flourish. To avoid conflict of interest, foreign legionaires were invariably posted far from their homeland. (The Ninth Legion, which disappeared in Caledonia, consisted of Spanish soldiers.) Consequently, legionaires felt increasingly bound to their commander, their loyalty invested in the man who led them and rewarded them with booty, rather than the rulers in distant Rome. The commander of a legion (*legatus*) held his post for up to four years, often passing on to a provincial governorship, where he could amass a substantial fortune. Charismatic commanders increasingly came to regard their troops as their own men. One such was Julius Caesar, whose life aptly parallels the last days of the Republic.

Julius Caesar was born into the nobility in 102 BC. Romans had long admired Greek learning, and in 75 BC Caesar was on his way to Rhodes to study oratory when he was captured by Aegean pirates. Insulted at the low ransom the pirates required for his freedom, he vowed to them that on his release he would hunt them down and crucify them – which he did. Through connections and ability, he quickly rose to become a political tribune. On a posting to Spain he saw a statue of Alexander the Great, prompting him to realise that at his age, Alexander had ruled the world. This spurred his already overweening ambition.

By 59 BC, he had been elected (by means of bribery) as a consul. Yet during his period of office, he sought to redistribute land amongst the poor. Such was typical of Caesar's character: both ruthless, yet true to his beliefs. His time as consul was followed by a series of military campaigns in which he proved himself the equal of any commander. His exploits included the first invasion of Britain (55 BC), building a bridge across the Rhine, and

an ultimately victorious series of campaigns against the
Gauls (58–50 BC). During the course of this bitterly fought
campaign, which included the loss and slaughter of a
Roman legion, Caesar is said to have despatched as many
as 100,000 slaves to Rome, helping to pay off the huge
debts he had accumulated in furthering his ambitions.

In 50 BC, Caesar was ordered to disband his army and
return to Rome to face charges of exceeding his orders.
Had Caesar returned alone, he would have faced criminal
prosecution, with his many enemies calling for his death.
Instead, he marched his 13th Legion back to Italy. By
marching across the Rubicon (a river in north-east Italy),
he entered Roman territory bearing arms, an act of treason
from which there was no going back. In the ensuing civil
war, he chased his rival Pompey to Egypt, where he hunted
down and killed his enemy. There then followed his celebrated affair with Cleopatra.

On his return to Rome, he assumed dictatorial powers.
He at once began instituting a number of much-needed
reforms, including a redistribution of land, pensions for
veterans, and in 45 BC the introduction of a new calendar.
Known as the Julian calendar, after its originator, this would
last for one and a half millennia; we still retain the same
names for the months, with July being named after Julius
Caesar. Other reforms included a concentration of power,
and bestowing upon himself the title 'dictator in perpetuity',
an honorific he would hold for just one month before he
was assassinated in March 44 BC.

The reign of Julius Caesar was a tipping point, signalling
the death throes of the Republic. As a man he was a
contradiction, emphasising many of the best, and the worst,
aspects of Ancient Rome. The most obvious, but often

overlooked of his qualities was his sheer intelligence. This was counter-balanced by his vanity, which ran the full gamut of his *amour propre* – from never forgetting a slight, to his constant worry over his receding hairline. Which brings us to his love life. Despite going through three wives, and juggling mistresses even in the midst of his most pressing campaigns, he is also known to have had a number of serious homosexual affairs, for which he suffered at the hands of the satirists and gossip-mongers in the senate.

Caesar's most noticeable characteristics were insatiable ambition and increasing megalomania, which were matched by his belief in the simple virtues of early Rome: physical and mental vigour, civic virtue and the like. He believed in reforms that would return Rome to these early glories, a cause which endeared him to his followers. His reforms endeared him to the plebs and middle classes, as well as a sizeable faction of the patricians. Many, such as the equally charismatic general Pompey, would later turn against him – whilst still retaining their admiration for his many skills. These included a military acumen on a par with Scipio, as well as highly developed and calculating political expertise.

He was also a fine, if unvarnished writer: his *Gallic Wars* contain precise (often self-serving) historical descriptions of his campaigns, and remain studied as classical texts to this day. He was also aware of the element of luck. The chances he took were often far more than calculated risks: he *dared* Fortuna, the goddess of luck. And he would certainly have seconded Napoleon's remark: 'I would rather have a lucky general than a good one.'

Looking back in history to the pre-Roman era, we can see that Caesar echoed many of the characteristics of those early rulers of empires, especially Alexander. Looking forward we can see uncanny echoes of his life and development in the many who would seek to emulate him – both seriously (Napoleon) and laughably (Mussolini).

A period of instability swept the Roman Empire, before Augustus took power in 27 BC as the first self-declared Emperor. This marks the beginning of the third period of Ancient Rome: the Empire, which would go through several transformations before its fall in AD 476. Ironically, the solid foundations of the Roman Empire were established well before the 'Empire' period, which mainly takes its name from the fact that it was ruled by an Emperor.

The first emperor Augustus was an adopted son of Julius Caesar, and would in time become known as Augustus Caesar. A precedent had been set: from now on the emperor would adopt his successor and bestow on him the name 'Caesar'. The original meaning of this name is obscure and disputed, but it may well refer to Julius Caesar's birth by Caesarean section, from the Latin word *caedere* 'to cut' (supine: *caesum*). Following on from the Roman emperors, the name would evolve into the Russian 'Czar', and the German 'Kaiser'. Resemblances to the earlier Babylonian Belshazzar and the Akkadian-Babylonian Nebuchadnezzar fall into the 'at best circumstantial and at worst non-existent' class of history. But as we have seen, such 'theories' will always flourish – with items like the Chinese discovery of Australia, and Erich von Däniken's *Chariots of the Gods*,[10] making regular appearances.

More interestingly, many fundamental cultural theories

---

10 This Swiss author made a name, and a fortune, for himself by claiming that religion and technology were given to ancient civilisations by extraterrestrials (seen as gods) arriving in spaceships (chariots).

held to be self-evidently true for centuries have also been relegated to this 'non-existent' class. Flat earthers and alchemists may have fallen foul of scientific investigation, but more plausibly supported theories remain vulnerable to newly discovered facts, or even simply a transformation of cultural outlook. In 1969, the British art historian Kenneth Clark delivered what was deemed at the time to be a definitive TV series named *Civilisation*. Almost half a century later, a series of programmes with similar grandiose ambitions, delivered by Mary Beard, Simon Schama and David Olugosa, would be named *Civilisations*, in the plural. This trio – an entertainingly erudite classicist, a British art historian of Jewish descent, and a British-Nigerian popular academic – extended their scope far beyond the Western tradition central to the patrician Clark's vision.

Their fresh world-view included examples across the ages from every inhabited continent. Here too was a transformation that quite matched the end of the flat earth era. The solid, self-evident, two-dimensional plane of a single progressive Western civilisation had been transformed into a three-dimensional globe of multi-cultural traditions. History will always remain fluid, open to fresh interpretation – spurred by the discovery of new facts, the evolution of new modes of thought.

In the Empire period, the population of the city of Rome is thought to have been somewhere between 320,000 and a million, while the empire it ruled over covered the equivalent area (though not the exact territory) of modern Europe, containing a population of between 50–90 million. The range and inexactitude of these figures is indicative: indeed, the word 'census' is derived from the Latin word *censere* (to estimate). Roman citizens, and those foreigners lucky enough to attain Roman citizenship, were granted a number of privileges – such as the right to vote, immunity from certain taxes, the right to defend themselves at a fully legal trial, and the right to live in Rome. Women and slaves were not counted as citizens, although their number may have blurred the census estimates. Women of child-bearing age were almost permanently pregnant, with unwanted babies left out on street corners.

Not for nothing was it said that 'all roads lead to Rome'. The characteristically straight Roman roads fanned out overland to the most distant parts of the empire. But they also attracted many to journey to the greatest city the world had yet seen. Curiously, this powerful urban centre did not actually produce anything. All goods, from grain to wine, nails to cloth, had to be imported – largely through the port of Ostia, some twenty miles south-west at the mouth of the Tiber. Here cargo arrived from all over the Mediterranean and beyond (grain from North Africa, tin from Cornwall, silk from China via the Levant); it was then transported up the Tiber on barges.

As the population of Rome began to swell, it became necessary to placate the common people, many of whom lived in crowded tenements and were left unemployed due to slavery. The authorities adopted a policy of *panem et circenses* ('bread and circuses'). This entailed free food and regular entertainments at the Colosseum, which took ten years to build (AD 70–80), and at its height was said to accommodate over 80,000 spectators. This staged such events as gladiatorial combats, malefactors being attacked and eaten by wild beasts, as well as occasional *naumachia* (mock naval battles). The latter were particularly popular, and pre-dated the building of the Colosseum.

The first of these was staged in 42 BC by Julius Caesar himself, in a large flooded pit beside the Tiber, estimated to have been some 500 yards long and 300 yards wide. This was a 'mock' battle only in the sense that it was staged – and on a huge scale. Several dozen vessels, including triremes (manned by galley slaves hauling three horizontal rows of banked oars), rammed their opponents prior to hand to hand fighting. Caesar's initial spectacle involved 2,000 'soldiers' and 4,000 'galley slaves'. Both 'soldiers' and 'slaves' consisted of prisoners-of-war and condemned criminals.

Such spectacles not only entertained the masses, allowing them to vent their blood lust, but also cowed them. Life was cheap, and authority was harsh to those who fell foul of it. Compare such entertainments with classical Greek theatre, held in amphitheatres, and attended by the population of a city state. Both forms had a cathartic element, but where one retold the ancient myths of its people (Oedipus and the like), the other was a demonstration of vicious brute force. One embodied art, democracy, and even psychological wisdom; the other indicated an increasingly rigid autocracy.

We may not know the exact populations of Rome and other cities in the empire, but owing to one of the greatest freak occasions in history, we can form a surprisingly precise picture of what life was like in such places. On 23 November AD 79,[11] the volcano Vesuvius in southern Italy erupted, covering the nearby town of Pompei in volcanic

---

11 In the eye-witness account written some years later by the lawyer and author Pliny the Younger, he stated that the eruption took place on 24 August. Recent excavations indicating the dried fruit and autumn vegetables available on the market stalls, as well as the warmer clothing worn by the inhabitants at the time, have prompted historians to reinterpret Pliny's date.

ash, preserving it largely intact for posterity. Houses, people, streets, wine jars, dogs even – all the bustle and variety of Roman life was immobilised in a long agonising moment. We can see pictures of the richer inhabitants in the precisely preserved frescoes on the walls of their villas; we can hear the gossip and scandal peddled by the common people in the graffiti ('Restitus was here', 'Handle with care' [beside an outline of a penis], 'Atimaeus made me pregnant'). There were even cartoons with speech bubbles on the walls of the taverns. We can tell what the inhabitants drank, how the rich banqueted, how citizens relieved themselves in communal rows of open lavatories, the illustrated service charges in the bordellos. All human life is here.

We can deduce from biblical references that things would have been only a little more primitive on the streets of ancient Babylon; likewise, we learn from the fifteenth-century French poet, François Villon, that things were only a little more sophisticated on the streets of medieval Paris. If we judge by mortality rates, the lives of the under-privileged throughout Europe and the Mediterranean region remained much the same until the nineteenth century. During the Babylonian era, life expectancy amongst the common population has been calculated at around twenty-six years, similarly in Roman times it was twenty-five years, and during the medieval era thirty years. Not until nineteenth-century England did this rise to forty years.

Admittedly, all such figures are difficult to gauge, and heavily disputed. Were they skewed by the inclusion of high child mortality rates? Just how much did they apply to the 'common people', rather than the population as a whole? Here again, the notion of census would seem to imply a large element of estimation. My point is that despite variations in population, exceptional plagues, wars and so forth, the condition of life for the poor remained for the most part barely above subsistence level throughout these eras.

On the other hand, there is no denying that the Roman Empire marked a great leap forward in human history. Where the Ancient Greeks made a fundamental theoretical contribution, the Roman contribution was largely practical. This is, of course, a huge generalisation. Greek architecture, with its epitome on the Acropolis at Athens, was a wonder to behold. Yet it was the Romans who added the final counter-intuitive practicality in the form of the keystone, which both completed and held together the gravity-defying stones of the arch. This great invention enabled the introduction of longer straight roads, with arched bridges, and finally aqueducts, some more than fifty miles long, often supported by as many as three stacked rows of arches.

Two thousand years later, some of these aqueducts are still in working order: the Trevi Fountain in modern Rome is supplied by water from the Virgo Aqueduct built by the Gallo-Roman general Agricola in 19 BC to supply water for the public baths. From this two-dimensional beginning would emerge the magnificence of the three-dimensional dome, another Roman marvel, which would not be emulated for almost a thousand years after the Fall of the Western Roman Empire. Yet not all Roman usages were a success. Greek mathematics was a sublime creation. Roman numerals, which all but eliminated the possibility of division or multiplication, soon put a stop to theoretical mathematics and other more practical mathematical advances.

Despite such glitches, the sheer organisation required to run an empire of such a scale continues to astonish. From Hadrian's Wall to Hadrian's Arch in the Middle East is just under 2,500 miles as the crow flies, or the Roman road would like to have travelled. (Around the same distance as from Miami to Los Angeles.) Yet the entire empire ran largely according to the dictates of a single centralised system.

An ancient Roman aqueduct

The currency was the same – based on the silver denarius. In times of severe shortage, the price of goods would be carved in stone (literally) at markets of the empire, to prevent traders from charging exorbitant prices. The economics of supply and demand was understood on a rule of thumb basis by the traders themselves, but its larger economic implications barely registered with the authorities. With so many dependent upon a subsistence level of supply, the flawed economics of slavery was irrelevant. (Pay workers and they spend, thus the economy grows.)

On the other hand, the Roman Legal Code would evolve over the years into a highly sophisticated system of jurisprudence. Our very word derives from the Latin: *juris, ius* (law, right), and *prudentia* (wisdom or knowledge). Roman law, from the original Twelve Tables of 449 BC to the *Corpus Juris Civilis* (Body of Civil Law) promulgated in AD 521, would provide the foundation for a host of legal systems to come. Its influence and distinctions are still recognisable in the framework of much Western law.

Yet the Roman Empire was not on the whole a happy place. When emperors began to assume the mantle of deity, and expected to be worshipped as such, the multi-theistic quasi-superstitious religion inherited from the Greeks gradually became sapped of its spirituality. The distinctly unholy behaviour of the likes of Tiberius, Caligula and Nero – now, as then, bywords for depravity – prompted belief in a new spirituality, unsullied by any connection with temporal power. It is no accident that the crucifixion of Jesus Christ took place during the reign of Tiberius – or that Nero made the Christians scapegoats for the Fire of Rome in AD 64. Yet this secret 'religion of slaves' would continue to flourish, until eventually the Emperor Constantine was converted in AD 313.

The last years of the Republic and the early years of the Empire would see Rome at its cultural zenith. Although the Romans produced no match for the sheer creative intelligence of the Ancient Greeks, their culture is certainly a noble echo, making up in sophistication for what it may lack in raw originality. To mention but a few examples. The poet Ovid wrote exquisite love poems and scurrilous satire, and was banished to the Black Sea for his troubles. Lucretius's great scientific poem, *De rerum natura* (On the Nature of Things), reintroduced the Greek philosopher Democritus's idea of the atom as the ultimate object of matter (from *a-tomos*, meaning 'un-cuttable', or 'indivisible').

The Greek physician Galen, who practised in Rome in the second century AD, established a body of medical knowledge that would last for almost one and a half millennia. The philosopher and dramatist Seneca wrote tragedies that would influence Shakespeare; and he also preached the philosophy of Stoicism, so popular amongst educated Romans, with its selfless message on how to endure adversity. Napoleon may have much admired Julius Caesar, but he refrained from reading about Ancient Rome, citing too much opening of veins. Suicide was prevalent amongst patricians who fell from favour, the prime exemplar being Seneca, who chose to open his veins rather than suffer the public disgrace of execution after he was accused of plotting against Nero.

The terminal decline of the Roman Empire began around the later third century AD, and would end with the sack of Rome in 410 by Alaric the Goth. This long gradual collapse has been ascribed to all manner of reasons – ranging from moral decay to gradual enfeeblement due to lead poisoning from the hot water pipes. Edward Gibbon, the eighteenth-century British author of the renowned six-volume *Decline and Fall of the Roman Empire*, blamed Christianity. Of all the many contributory factors, one stands out: the mass migration across Europe of warrior tribes such as the Goths, the Vandals and the Huns. These would seem to have been irresistible by an empire beset with civil war, plague and economic decline.

Yet the fall of Rome did not mark the extinction of the Roman Empire. By the fourth century, the Emperor Constantine had moved the capital to Byzantium, soon to be named Constantinople after him (now Istanbul). This would split off to become an Eastern Empire, which managed to hold out as the Germanic tribes and their followers overran the rest of the Western Empire. The Eastern Empire would gradually take on the tenor, as well as the name, of its capital city – becoming the Byzantine Empire. The Roman Empire, as such, was no more.

Sequence

'What have the Romans ever done for us?' The answer to this question became most apparent when the Romans departed, leaving behind dilapidated outpost forts, abandoned stretches of aqueduct leading from nowhere to nowhere, villas with crumbling mosaic floors undermined by defunct heating systems, and buried pouches of gold coins that would remain undiscovered until the age of the metal detector.

It is during this period, between the sixth and eighth centuries, that the lack of communication between provinces of the former empire caused the vulgar Latin used throughout the Roman Empire to split into what became known as the Romance languages, such as French, Italian and Spanish, which are spoken today. The term Dark Ages is now frowned upon by serious historians, yet it certainly evokes much of the period between the Fall of Rome and the tenth century. Instead, many choose to call this period 'Late Antiquity' or the 'Early Medieval Era', preferring to reference the two ages that bookend its years. Paradoxically, this dark age was a period of both cultural stagnation and mass migration.

The movement of peoples had begun with the migration of the nomadic Hun tribes from Eastern Asia across the steppes westwards into Europe. This set in motion a disturbance that would spread throughout the continent. In the face of the advancing Huns, the Germanic tribes were forced to migrate south from their homelands. In waves the Goths (originally from Sweden and Eastern Germany) swept through Eastern Europe, splitting into the Visigoths and the Ostrogoths as they passed through Southern Europe and along the shores of North Africa. The Germanic and proto-Slavic Vandals swept through France, Spain and North Africa; while the Huns (from Central Asia and the Caucasus) migrated through Hungary, France and the Balkans.

Later the Vikings (from Scandinavia) sailed to attack the shores of all northern Europe, eventually travelling as far as Greenland and the New World. Other Vikings sailed down the Volga, increasingly as traders, establishing the state of Rus, before venturing south across the Black Sea to arrive at Byzantium. Out of this chaos, in 800 Charlemagne established a Frankish Empire, which briefly ruled over much of western Europe. Meanwhile the Byzantine Empire continued to wax and wane over Anatolia and the Balkans. By now this remnant of Roman rule had become, both in culture and language, a largely Greek empire. Ancient Rome, as such, was now but a reference point in history.

Meanwhile the mantle of progress passed further east. The scattered books and learning of the classical era were taken up, and developed, by Arab scholars, in a second flourishing of Middle Eastern civilisation. Just as Christianity would receive its founding inspiration from the historical

Jesus of Nazareth, so Islam would be founded by the prophet Muhammad. Islam recognised itself as following on from the two previous monotheistic religions of the Middle East, namely Judaism and Christianity. The Judaic Abraham and Moses, as well as Christ, were all seen as earlier prophets, predecessors of the Final Prophet of God, Muhammad. But here the resemblance ends. Muhammad was no Jesus Christ, and the empire he founded was based on no 'religion of slaves'. The empire of Muhammad was the empire of a fervent new religion; and was, from its outset, an empire of conquest.

3

The Umayyad and
Abbasid Caliphates

For many Western minds, the stereotypical image of the Arab caliphates is exemplified by Scheherazade, the condemned storyteller who managed to stay alive by entrancing the Sultan of Baghdad for one thousand and one nights. Such were her fabulous and magical stories that at the end of each night, the Sultan postponed her execution so that he could hear the end of the current story, which had been interrupted by the rising of the dawn.

The name Scheherazade is of Persian origin, and her tales of the likes of Ali Baba, Sinbad the Sailor and Aladdin run the gamut of the oriental world. Aladdin, for instance, despite his Arabic name (Ala ad-Din), is from China – or at least an Arabic-medieval version of this land. And the sorcerer who befriends Aladdin hails from the Barbary Coast of North Africa, the westernmost Islamic territory half a world away from China. The blend of exoticism, ancient wonder and the ever-present threat of death creates an imaginative never-never land, whose many-coloured glass stains the white radiance of historical actuality.

This latter has come down to us in such words as algebra, alcohol and alchemy (which despite its illusory aim developed many of the laboratory techniques and material distinctions of modern chemistry). In these words, the prefix al-, as also in algorithm, is the give-away. But our language, and our knowledge, is peppered with a variety of other borrowings from Arabic. Ranging through Admiral (Emir) to zero (which would transform western European mathematics), through coffee, cotton and cork, to gauze, soda and traffic, the list goes on and on. This verbal heritage hints at the host of more realistic advances bequeathed by the era of the caliphates, when once again this Middle Eastern corner of the globe led all civilisations.

In order to grasp the rationale of the caliphates, we must first understand their religion and the import of its founder. Muhammad was born into a leading family at Mecca in western central Arabia, during the 'Year of the Elephant', reckoned to be around AD 570. His father died before his birth, and his mother died when he was six, leaving him to be brought up by a paternal uncle, Abu Talib, and his wife. When Muhammad was a young man, he travelled as a merchant to Syria, and later became involved in trade between the Indian Ocean and the Mediterranean, where he gained a reputation as a truthful and trustworthy man, whose advice was often sought in the resolution of disputes. But he also had a deep spiritual side. Each year he would retire to a mountain cave outside Mecca to meditate and pray.

In AD 610, when he was forty years old, the angel Gabriel appeared to him, and passed on to him verses that would later become part of the Quran, a book which would come to be regarded as the word of God. Later, Muhammad would begin preaching, according to the revelations of God's word conveyed to him by Gabriel: 'God is one' and *islam* 'submission'. This was largely unsuccessful, as the inhabitants of Mecca were polytheistic, with each tribe having its own god or protector. Consequently, Muhammad and his followers migrated some fifty miles north to Medina in AD 622, which marks the first year of the Muslim calendar.

Here, after leading his followers through several years of armed struggle, Muhammad gathered 10,000 of his men and marched successfully on Mecca. In 632, he returned on a final pilgrimage to Mecca, thus establishing a tradition known as the *Hadj*, the annual pilgrimage to Mecca, which should be undertaken once in a lifetime by all adult Muslims. Months after his return to Medina, Muhammad died at the age of sixty-two. By this time, a large part of the Arabian peninsula had been converted to Islam.

The harsh desert conditions of Arabia dictated a simple life, where a close communal existence was essential for survival. The purity, loyalty and fervent adherence to a common belief required of such a life would be embodied in the Five Pillars of Wisdom central to Islamic faith: *Shahada* (to profess that there is no God but Allah, and that Muhammad is the messenger of Allah), *Salat* (performance of ritual prayer five times a day), *Zakat* (giving alms to the poor), *Sawm* (fasting during the month of Ramadan), and *Hadj* (pilgrimage to Mecca). These appear in the Hadith, words spoken by Muhammad, but only written down after his death. The Quran and the Hadith form the basis of Muslim law, often known as *sharia* law.

Following Muhammad's death, the Rashidun Caliphate

was established, with its leader (caliph) being chosen by a democratic consultation amongst elders, or according to the wishes of his predecessor. The fourth caliph was Ali, the cousin and son-in-law of Muhammad, the first to be a direct blood-descendant of the Prophet. As such, Ali is regarded as Muhammad's rightful successor by all Shia Muslims. (The name Shia derives from *Shiat Ali* 'partisans of Ali'.) Sunni Muslims recognise his three predecessors.

The Rashidun Caliphate (632–661) would include a twenty-four-year period of rapid military expansion, with Muslim Arabs completing their conquest of the entire Arabian peninsula, before spreading east across Persia. Ensuing caliphates overran territory as far as Armenia and modern-day Afghanistan, at the same time spreading west through Egypt and later the littoral of North Africa as far as Tunisia. What accounts for the success of this rapid expansion, which would continue after Ali died in 661, and the consequent establishment of the Umayyad Caliphate?

The initial important factor was Muhammad's move from Mecca to Medina. Not for nothing is this seen as year one of the Muslim calendar. By moving away from Mecca, Muhammad and his followers loosened their tribal loyalties and developed a close communal bond, all defending each other against the hostility they encountered from surrounding believers in other tribal gods. It soon became clear to Muhammad that aggression was necessary for survival. At the same time, this also helped gain converts.

If Islam was to become more than a local cult in Medina, and to fulfil the promise of its core belief in a single God, it needed to expand. The belief in a single all-powerful deity renders any who believe in different gods nothing less than heretics opposed to the one true faith, who must be shown the error of their ways. As a former trader, Muhammad well understood the logistics of economic survival. His initial expansion beyond Medina involved cutting the supply lines to the inland desert cities, which relied upon caravans from the coast.

As the number of converts to this single-minded religion increased, so did their fervent belief in themselves. Again and again in history, it will be seen how a well-directed army fired by a belief in its own cause, which instils self-lessness and an iron discipline, can produce an all but unstoppable force. (Just over a thousand years later, an ill-equipped French army, its soldiery inspired by a belief in the Revolution, would conquer Europe.)

The remnant Persian Empire (Sassanid), and the far-flung eastern edges of the Byzantine Empire, proved no match for the zealous Arabs, who quickly absorbed them, introducing their language and beliefs to new lands. The ruler Ali would transfer the capital of the caliphate to Kufa in Iraq, which was more strategically placed to rule the expanding empire. However, by the end of his five-year caliphate, a civil war had broken out between the Sunni faction, and Ali's Shia faction, which recognised him as the only true successor to Muhammad, by way of the bloodline. In 661, whilst Ali was praying at the Great Mosque of Kufa, he was assassinated. This led to the establishment of the second caliphate, which was ruled by the Umayyad Dynasty, who were Sunnis. The first ruler of this caliphate was Muawiya, who had been the governor of Syria, and his first move was to transfer the capital to Damascus.

Despite such internal conflicts, the expansion of the caliphate continued under the Umayyad dynasty. The most notable new conquest was the expansion along the north African coast, and the invasion of the Iberian peninsula, which was at the time occupied by Visigoth Christian kingdoms. Regardless of the Islamic zeal of the conquerors, they remained mindful of Muhammad's explicit command with regard to members of the Abrahamic faith. This included both Jews and Christians. According to Muhammad, these should be permitted to continue practising their faith, as long as they paid the *jizyah* tax, a tribute payable annually to the Muslim authorities. This was usually assessed on the ability of the person to pay, and was invariably more or less greater than the local Muslims paid as part of their *zakat* (the Third Pillar of Wisdom, concerning alms to the poor).

Similarly, Christian and Jewish communities were permitted to continue operating according to their own legal systems, leaving them largely autonomous within the caliphate. For this reason, the Umayyad Caliphate may be regarded as a secular state: that is, government was separated from religious authority. In other words, Sharia Law – derived from the Quran and Hadith (sayings of Muhammad) – was not applied throughout the civil sphere.

Such freedom inevitably resulted in certain anomalies. For instance, as the caliphate expanded beyond the borders of Syria into Anatolia, it found itself fighting the Byzantine Christians. Meanwhile, the many Christians within the borders of Syria were not regarded as the enemy, and were permitted to go about their business as before. Even more astonishing is the fact that Muawiya, the first caliph of the Umayyad dynasty, was even married to a Christian. Despite such apparent contradictions, in practice this policy only served to strengthen and consolidate Umayyad rule in the new territories. Here we can see that they were in accord with the twentieth-century historian Paul Kriwaczek's insight that empires which allow a certain freedom to their subject peoples tend to be more easy to control and last longer.

The conquest of the Iberian peninsula, along with expansion east as far as the Aral Sea and modern-day Pakistan, left the Umayyad Caliphate ruling over a vast region covering around 4,300,000 square miles, and 62 million people. (At the time a third of the world's population.) This was the largest empire the world had yet seen – around twice the size of the Roman Empire at its zenith.[12]

By 711, the Umayyad conquest of the Iberian peninsula was complete, and Arab forces now pushed across the Pyrenees, spreading east along the coast of southern France, and north into the heartland of France itself. The Umayyads continued to sweep all before them until in October 732 they reached as far north as Tours, less than 150 miles south-west of Paris. It seemed as if all western Europe lay at their mercy.

However, they now found themselves opposed by the combined forces of Charles Martel, ruler of the Franks, and Odo the Great of Aquitaine.[13] The appearance of

---

12 This may appear not to be the case when the two empires are compared on modern maps. Such maps are made according to Mercator's projection, which exaggerates the area of the regions further from the equator. In actuality, Greenland is the same size as modern-day Algeria, whereas on Mercator's projection Greenland appears as large as the entire continent of Africa, i.e. fourteen times larger than it is in reality.

13 Odo's origins are obscure. Some claim he may have been of Roman lineage, others have suggested he was a Hun or a Visigoth.

Martel and the Franks in such numbers caught the Umayyad general Abd-al-Rahman by surprise, and Martel formed a square, taking advantage of the hills and woods as cover. Opinions differ as to which side had the largest army, but there is no doubt that Martel had been preparing for this battle for some years. The fearsome Umayyad cavalry was forced to charge uphill through trees; meanwhile their infantry was ill-dressed for the cold French autumn. Martel's eventual victory sent the Umayyad army into retreat back across the Pyrenees.

In the words of the great nineteenth-century German historian, von Ranke, this battle 'was the turning point of one of the greatest epochs of European history.' Instead of western Europe becoming an Arab continent, it now meant that Frankish power was established. Within less than forty years, Charlemagne ('Charles the Great') would be crowned king of the Franks, and set about establishing an empire that unified much of western Europe for the first time since the Fall of Rome.

The Umayyad Caliphate would continue to rule until it came into conflict with the Abbasid revolution in 750. The Umayyad forces under their White Flag were soon overcome by the Black Flag of the Abbasids and a new caliphate was established.[14] The Abbasid family was descended from Muhammad's uncle Abbas ibn Abd al-Muttallib, after whom they were named. So once again, this was a Sunni dynasty, as their caliphs were not directly descended from

---

14 By this stage many of those fighting for the Umayyads were Shiites. To this day, the Shiites retain their favour for the White Flag, whereas Sunni Muslims swear allegiance to the Black Flag, said to have been the one favoured by Muhammad.

the Prophet. The Abbasid power base was Persia, and soon after they assumed power, the capital would be transferred to Baghdad. This was to be the beginning of the Golden Age of Islam, when the originally Arab world of the caliphates would take on a distinctly Persian hue.

Most famous of its early caliphs was undoubtedly Harun al-Rashid ('Harun the Rightly Guided'), who features as the sultan in the *One Thousand and One Nights* of Scheherazade. From the outset, the Abbasid caliphs saw it as their duty to promote learning, founding the House of Wisdom. This probably began as the large private library of Harun al-Rashid, which he made available to scholars. It soon evolved into an intellectual centre of learning, attracting scholars of the highest quality.

The most significant of its early functions was the sponsoring of the Translation Movement, which would have a major influence on Arabic thought over the coming six centuries of the caliphate. This movement was responsible for translating works of the Ancient Greek mathematicians, physicians, astronomers and philosophers (especially Aristotle). Many of these works had been lost in the West after the Fall of the Roman Empire, and the effect of this new knowledge upon Arabic thought cannot be over-estimated. It certainly influenced some of the finest minds of the caliphate period. But more than this, it inspired them to original thinking, which was in advance of anything hitherto found in human knowledge.

Two incidents serve to illustrate the significance of this to the outside world. In 802 Charlemagne sent a mission of friendship to the court of Harun al-Rashid. This returned with a gift for the King of the Franks, in the form of a gilded bronze clock – at a time when no such thing existed throughout Europe. According to the modern French historian André Clot, this clock was 'a clepsydra, which on the hour sounded a chime and dropped small coloured balls into a pool; at midday twelve horsemen galloped out of twelve windows in the case.' Charlemagne and his courtiers gazed in awe at this wondrous instrument, convinced that it worked by conjuring up magical spirits.

The second incident took place some 300 years later, when an English philosopher and traveller named Adelard of Bath returned from a voyage to the Levant, where he had scarcely been able to believe what he had seen and learned. The Arabs had translated hitherto unknown works of Aristotle and the Ancient Greeks, thus immeasurably increasing their learning – especially in the field of natural philosophy (what we would now call science).

They had gone on to achieve amazing feats, such as measuring the circumference of the earth (a feat achieved by the ancient Greeks, but subsequently forgotten). Muslim scholars had also invented algebra, and drawn diagrams of how the human body worked. They had discovered new curative ointments and medicines, and had created an astrolabe that could measure the movements of the stars. This latter had enabled the Arabs to make new discoveries in astronomy, and vastly improved their ability to navigate when travelling by sea or across deserts.

Other Western visitors would confirm Adelard's fabulous stories, even adding to them. One told of a battle in the far north-east of the caliphate, where the Muslims had taken a number of prisoners-of-war, who had subsequently passed on a secret of their oriental culture: how to make paper out of rags, which could then be written on. (This is now reckoned to refer to the Battle of Talas, which took place in Kazakhstan in 751, the only known conflict between Abbasid and Chinese armies.)

So who were these great Arab thinkers? What exactly was the import of their discoveries? And how did they manage to accomplish such feats? The general answer to the last question much resembles the explanation for the sudden explosion of learning in Ancient Greece. That is, the separation of religious and scientific thought. The scientists declared that all learning, both spiritual and secular, was 'understanding the mind of God'. Anyone who sought to curtail their researches was thus committing blasphemy. Fortunately, it was several centuries before the religious authorities saw a way around this sophistry, which usurped their all-embracing powers.

The treatment of the sick in the courtyards of mosques dated back as far as Muhammad himself and his mosque in Medina. Such places gradually became separate institutions, known as *bimaristan*, a Persian word for 'home of the sick'. The first great *bimaristan* was founded in 805 by Harun al-Rashid in Baghdad. Within the first decades of the Abbasid Caliphate, other hospitals had been established in Cairo, Damascus and Cordoba. The religious influence remained in the fact that all – regardless of sex, race or religion – could be treated at such institutions, and free of charge.

On the other hand, the knowledge and practices employed in such hospitals was purely secular. Arab medical scholars made use of the translated works of Aristotle, and in particular Galen. Another religious aspect of such places was the belief that 'God sends down no malady without also sending down with it a cure'. Such a belief might not be scientific, but it was certainly an inspiration to those studying medicine, who immediately set about seeking cures for the ailments with which they were confronted. As we shall see, one of the reasons for this golden age was that although religion and science were separate, they actually supported one another. Science was a religious quest, inspired by religious belief.

The first great scholar to embody this tradition was Al-Razi (often known as Rhazes in the West), who was born in 854 in Ray, south of the Caspian Sea in Persia. He travelled to Baghdad as a young man, where such was the depth and breadth of his intellect that he was asked by the Abbasid caliph al-Mutadid to found a new great hospital, intended to be the finest and greatest in all the caliphate. An indication of Al-Razi's scientific thought can be seen in the method he used to choose the hospital's location. He selected the district where the fresh meat displayed on the hooks outside the butchers' stalls took the longest to rot.

Al-Razi would complete over two hundred manuscripts during the course of his sixty-five-year lifetime. In common with other scholars of the day, he did not limit himself to one field. His greatest advances may have been in medicine, where he wrote pioneering work on contagious diseases and anatomy, but he also made original contributions to fields from logic to astronomy, grammar and philosophy.

The Baghdad of this era was one of the wonders of the world. Sailing ships from as far afield as Cathay (China) and Zanzibar tied up at the palm-fringed quays along the Euphrates river. At the heart of Baghdad lay the famed two-mile-wide Round City, with its three rings of defensive walls, within which stood the Golden Palace of the caliphs and the Grand Mosque. From here four axial roads ran out to the four corners of the Arabic Empire. In suburbs beyond the walls were villas with shaded gardens and tinkling fountains. Beyond lay the teeming bazaars whose stalls displayed cinnamon from Sumatra, cloves from Zanzibar and a plethora of goods in between. On the streets, entertainments ranged from fire-eaters and sword-swallowers to turbanned storytellers, recounting many of the same tales that appear in *One Thousand and One Nights*.

But these magical narratives were far from being the only great literature produced during this golden era. Perhaps best known in the West is *The Rubaiyat of Omar Khayyam*, which would cause a sensation when it was translated some 700 years later by the Victorian English poet, Edward Fitzgerald. Omar Khayyam himself remains a somewhat mysterious figure, who achieved renown in his lifetime as an astronomer and a mathematician. His *Rubaiyat* (poems in quatrains) first appeared in a biography written about him over forty years after his death.

Since then as many as two thousand quatrains have been attributed to him. Though some of these are certainly not his work, there is no doubting the quality of the poetry itself:

Here with a Loaf of Bread beneath the Bough,
A Flask of Wine, a Book of Verse – and Thou
Beside me singing in the Wilderness –
And Wilderness is Paradise enow.

This was hardly the orthodox way to Paradise, and Omar Khayyam soon found himself facing a charge of impiety, whereupon he took the precaution of leaving town on a pilgrimage.

One of the great scholars of the Abbasid Caliphate was Muhammad al-Khwarizmi, who in 820 was appointed head librarian at the House of Wisdom in Baghdad. Al-Khwarizmi would produce works on astronomy, geography, and also mathematics. The last field would see his most permanent contributions. It was he who popularised the Hindu-Arabic numerals, which introduced a decimal counting system that freed mathematics from previous cumbersome methods of calculation.

His name, al-Khwarizmi, has come down to us in the word algorithm (a process or set of general rules for solving specific problems). But most important of all was his work *The Book on Calculation*, whose Arabic title contains the words *al-jabr* meaning 'the reunion of broken parts'. This is a penetrating metaphorical description of how we solve an equation with unknown quantities, and is the Arabic from which we derive the word 'algebra'.

In the Hadith, Muhammad explicitly forbade figurative representation, in case this led to idol worship. Consequently, Arabic art became sublimated into highly abstract forms such as patterned tiles and calligraphy. The walls of mosques – both great and small – contained superb examples of these Islamic forms of artistry. Here, in calligraphy, language and prayer took on a combined beauty of their own, whilst tiles exhibited complex geometric patterns and ingenious intricate symmetries that still intrigue mathematicians to this day.

Muhammad even taught his daughter Fatima calligraphy, and this practice was taken up by many women within the confines of the harem. Cut off from normal socialising, some of these women studied and became scholars in their own right. These scholars became renowned as teachers of women students. Little mention is made of such educated women, owing to the oppressive patriarchy of the society. However, we catch a tantalising glimpse in one of the tales related by Scheherazade.

Briefly, the story tells of how an Arab slave girl called Tawaddud was offered to the caliph, but her owner wanted him to pay an extortionate sum on account of her exceptional learning. To test this, the caliph summoned to his palace all the most learned men in the land, so that they could question her. First a scholar of the Quran began questioning her, and she gave correct answers to all his questions. Then she asked him a question, which he could not answer. The caliph ordered that the scholar be stripped of his robes and cast out in disgrace. Next a physician questioned her on details of anatomy and medicine. Tawaddud correctly answered all his questions, even apparently citing works of Galen as her authority. The physician was forced to concede to the caliph: 'This damsel is more learned than I in medicine.'

Finally, a philosopher questioned her on the nature of time, admitting defeat when she solved a mathematical riddle he posed. The caliph then offered to pay 100,000 gold pieces for Tawaddud, at the same time offering to grant her any request she chose. She replied that she wanted to return to her master, whereupon the caliph rewarded them both with a place at his court.

In 1095, the Eastern Mediterranean coast of the Abbasid Caliphate began coming under attack from the western armies of the Crusaders. These had been ordered by Pope Urban II to go to the assistance of the Byzantine Emperor, who was under threat from the Seljuk Turks (Sunni allies of the Abbasids). The Frankish warriors of the First

Crusade then invaded the Holy Land of their Christian heritage. By 1099 they had conquered Jerusalem and soon set up permanent Christian kingdoms along the hinterland of the eastern Mediterranean. Only when Salah ad-Din (Saladin), a Sunni Muslim of Kurdish descent, led the Islamic armies would the Crusaders meet their match, with Jerusalem being retaken in 1187.

By now the Abbasid Caliphate was beginning to fall apart, with various regions becoming virtually autonomous. Then, without warning, in 1257 a vast army of Mongols suddenly poured into Abbasid territory from the north-east, sweeping all before them. By January 1258, Baghdad itself was under siege. The following month the city was overrun, sacked and burnt to the ground.

From this time on, the centre of power in the Islamic Levant would move east to Cairo, where an Abbasid Caliphate would soon be re-established. But the golden era of the Baghdad Caliphate was over. The caliphs now only held religious power, with the resident Mamlukes holding the political and military power.

Despite this blow, one part of the old Islamic Empire continued to flourish. For years, Al-Andalus (the Iberian peninsula) had been a virtually autonomous province of the empire, ruled over by the Emir of Cordoba. Indeed, such was the independence of the Emirate of Cordoba that it retained its allegiance to the old Umayyad Caliphate. And soon its cultural magnificence had even begun to rival that of Abbasid Baghdad. By as early as the tenth century, the city of Cordoba had grown to an estimated population of 500,000, making it the largest city in Europe. (In the Empire, only Baghdad, and possibly Cairo, were larger, the former having a population of around 800,000.) With a mix of Islamic, Christian and Jewish people living in comparative harmony, Cordoba had become a great financial, political and cultural centre.

Even the second city of this independent emirate became a wonder of Islamic Europe. Granada, located almost 2,500 feet up in the cool Sierra Nevada, with its fabled Alhambra palace and gardens, would in time become independent of Cordoba. In this way, Granada was able to provide trade links between the Arabic world and the Christian provinces that were gradually making inroads into Al-Andalus in the north. This trade link reached south across the Mediterranean to the Berber territories of North Africa, and thence across the Sahara. (Sahara is simply the Arabic word for desert.)

These trade links carried caravans of gold from the mines of Mali, as well as salt, ivory and slaves north from Timbuktu. In the opposite direction, this trade route was also responsible for the spread of the Islamic religion to West Africa. Later, Granada would become a great centre of Jewish civic influence and culture, until the delicate balance of multi-religious tolerance was upset, resulting in the 1066 massacre of the Jews.

Al-Andalus would produce one of the greatest philosophers of the Arabic Golden age. This was Ibn Rushd, who was born in Cordoba in 1126. Like so many of the other great Arabic scholars of this era he was a polymath, writing works on everything from physics to jurisprudence. He travelled to Marrakesh, in the Islamic province of Morocco, where he made astronomical observations attempting unsuccessfully to discover physical laws that might explain the movement of the stars in the heavens. In later life he was appointed as a *qadi* (judge of the Sharia court) in Cordoba, but fell out of favour and was banished by the emir.

He is best remembered for his voluminous commentaries on the works of Aristotle. Many of these would be translated into Latin and began circulating amongst scholars in Europe. Here Ibn Rushd's name became Westernised to Averroes. Such was his influence on Medieval Christian thought that it led to a philosophy known as Averroism. This included a mystical strain, which claimed that all humanity shared the same eternal consciousness.

The Moroccan province was also the birthplace in 1304 of Ibn Battuta, the Islamic scholar who became the greatest traveller the world had yet seen. The extent of his travels, by camel, horse and boat continues to astonish to this day.

According to his verified account, his voyages would range east around India as far as China, south beyond Timbuktu, along the coast of East Africa beyond Zanzibar, and north around the Black Sea and the Caspian. In other words, Ibn Battuta travelled the length and breadth of the known world – or the extent of the world that was known to Arab traders. And this is the point. Before being a religious and military leader, Muhammad had been a trader. And after the early conquests, the Arab Muslims merely continued in this trading tradition, both by land, and especially by sea.

The most far-flung points that Ibn Battuta reached were already part of the Muslim world. For instance, Muslim traders first reached China as early as the seventh century, with the religion soon establishing itself amongst the local people. Similarly, the Berber traders crossing the Sahara from North Africa first brought Islam to sub-Saharan

Africa in the ninth century, when with the aid of missionaries it soon began to supplant the local African religions
in Mali and a wide swathe of territory reaching from
Senegal to the Sudan.

During the period when Ibn Battuta was travelling the
world, Christian forces continued pressing further and
further south through Al-Andalus. The last Arabic strong-
hold to fall was the Emirate of Granada in 1492. But this
was far from the end of Islamic power in Europe. In a
counterbalancing movement, the Ottoman Caliphate had
prevailed in Anatolia, finally conquering Constantinople,
the capital of the Byzantine Empire in 1453, before pressing
on into the Balkans. But the story of this great empire is
yet to come.

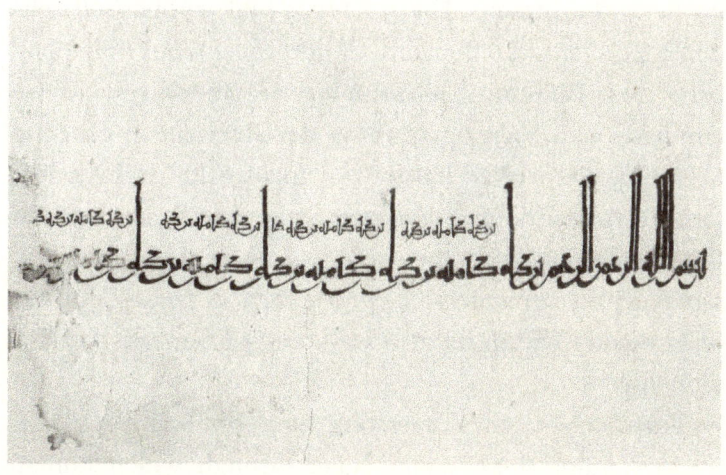

Page of Arabic script from the Abbasid era.

Sequence

As we have seen, by now the earliest centres of civilisation in Asia and North Africa – Ancient Egypt, Mesopotamia, the Indus Valley, and the Yellow River – had spread across their separate regions and gone on to become linked to each other through trade routes. In the era prior to this, they had developed largely in isolation. Yet around the fifth century BC, these entirely separate civilisations had reached a surprisingly similar stage of human evolution. They had each produced an exceptional figure of such stature that he would transform the intellectual development of his peoples for centuries, even millennia to come.

China had produced Confucius, whose ideas would continue to play a formative role in Chinese thought right down to the present. His teachings had emphasised self-development with the aim of improvement. India had produced Buddha, the founder of Buddhism, whose emphasis had been on spiritual development in order to overcome the wicked illusions of this world. And Ancient Greece had produced Socrates, who had instructed his followers to question themselves in order to know themselves. Quite separately, it seems, each of these branches of humanity had in its own way evolved a means to individuality.

This leads to the interesting question: was such self-understanding a necessary stage through which human evolution was bound to pass? Indeed, was this part of our common humanity? This is difficult to answer, for the simple reason that not all civilisations would sustain the means for such an attainment to flourish. Self-reflection was a luxury for the few, at the best of times. During more harsh periods, it would seem to be all but eradicated, in the cause of a powerful collectivism that claimed an overwhelming benefit for the common good. We have seen how an idea, or a new religion, can galvanise a people. Not for nothing does the word religion come from the Latin *re ligare*, 'the thing which binds us'.

The next empire we encounter will have a similarly powerful driving force, harking back to an almost pre-invidualistic collectivism. In so doing, we return to the empire that overran Baghdad in 1258, putting an end to the glories of the Abbasid Caliphate.

4

The Mongol Empire

Just as the Huns, the Goths and the Vandals had driven all before them some eight centuries previously, so would the Mongols prove an irresistible force as they spread out from their homeland across the Eurasian land mass.

In migrant tribes of hunter-gatherers, living off the land through which they passed, every man was a warrior. Such migrations could support roaming bands of a few hundred people at most. The next stage of human development involved shepherds. In such societies too, every man was a warrior; but as the warriors brought their sustenance with them in herds, they could move in larger groups. This was how Muhammad could gather 10,000 men for his march on Mecca.

The third stage of development involved settled pastoral people. Such societies were more sophisticated. The surplus of their produce could support leisure and culture – as well as a standing army. Yet ironically, these cultured societies were no match for the migrations of what were essentially barbarian tribesmen, as the Romans discovered. And now, almost a millennium later, the peoples of the Eastern and the Western worlds would be forced to learn this lesson anew – as the Mongol hordes poured out from their eastern fastness across two continents.[15]

No great empire is fundamentally unique – but the Mongol Empire would contain sufficient anomalies to set it apart from almost all other empires, both before and since, great and small. Its history, even its very existence, is beset with contradictions. This would be the largest contiguous land empire the world has ever seen, stretching from the Pacific to the eastern borders of Germany, yet it would prove the most short-lived great empire in history. It would be an empire that tolerated all religions – from Islam to Christianity and Buddhism, from Shamanism to Judaism and Taoism. Yet it would also forbid many of these religions from carrying out their most sacred practices.

For instance, followers of Islam were forbidden to slaughter meat in the halal manner; likewise, Jews were forbidden to eat kosher and practise circumcision. All citizens of the Mongol Empire had to follow 'the Mongol method of eating'. Similarly, the Mongol edicts against polluting water, which precluded the washing of clothes, or even bodies, particularly during summer, hardly endeared them to religions that held a strong connection between purity and godliness, with an abhorrence of the unclean.

Other similar contradictions abounded. Despite the vast area of its conquests, the Mongol Empire would leave

---

15 The eighteenth-century Scottish philosopher and pioneer of economics, Adam Smith, suggested that had the Native Americans reached the stage of becoming herdsmen, they would probably have succeeded in driving the first pastoral European settlers from their shores.

scattered ruins and no great buildings; the only magnificent monument that the Mongols caused to be created was the Great Wall of China, which had been intended to keep the Mongols *out*. This was an empire notorious for the vast slaughter it inflicted on its enemies; yet it would leave behind in Europe a legacy that caused an even greater death toll, in the form of the Black Death.

Even its emperors present us with a conundrum. Its first emperor, Genghis Khan, would go down in history as probably the most bloodthirsty conqueror of all time, an often genocidal invader who swept into oblivion those in his path. Yet the last ruler of the Mongol Empire is remembered in the romantic imagination of the West for his fabulous capital, Xanadu. This would be described by the contemporary English traveller, Samuel Purchas:

In Xanadu did Cublai Can build a stately Pallace, encompassing sixteen miles of plaine ground with a wall, wherein are fertile Meadowes, pleasant Springs, delightful Streames and all sorts of beasts of chase and game, and in the middest thereof a sumptuous house of pleasure which may be moved from place to place.[16]

Now all that remains of Xanadu are ruins circumscribed by a grassy mound where the city walls once stood. Yet Kublai Khan was to be no Ozymandias. In later life he would leave Xanadu and set up his capital in Khanbaliq (Mongolian: 'The City of the Leader') on the site of what is now the capital city of China: namely, Beijing. Many

---

16 Reminiscent of the Mongolian nomadic life, where tribespeople inhabited a moveable *ger* (a felt or skin tent, like a yurt).

centuries have come and gone, yet this city and its great monuments have yet to lie in shattered remnants amidst the lone and level sands.

To the north of China, beyond the famously treacherous shifting singing sands of the Gobi desert, and hemmed in by mountains to the north and the west, lie the vast grassy steppes of the landlocked territory known as Mongolia. This plateau is around 5,000 feet above sea level, and stretches some 1,500 miles from east to west, and more than 500 miles from north to south. It has been occupied by nomadic tribesmen since time immemorial. (Historians estimate this as being since around 2000 BC.) The origin myths of these people were entirely vocal, and over the centuries they have become muddled with Buddhist and Shamanistic folklore from surrounding peoples. But one thing remained certain, these tribal nomads regarded the wolf as their legendary ancestor, and they strove to emulate his qualities: cunning, ferocity and the strength of the pack.[17]

The Mongols may have identified themselves with the wolf, but the one animal these tribesmen cherished above all others was the horse. Mongolian horses were (and remain to this day) a sturdy, stocky breed of amazing endurance. Wandering free, they subsist on grass alone, and are able to withstand the extremes of temperature that

---

17 The recurrence of the wolf in fundamental mythologies is widespread, if not universal. It stretches from Gilgamesh and Akkadian myth to Rome, from Norse mythology to Beowolf, even into New World Inuit and Cherokee legends. Some point to the wolf being the most feared predator faced by early humans; however, the underlying identification with wolves would seem to indicate some deeper psychological atavism.

characterise this otherwise empty region. In summer, the heat rises to over 30°C, in winter it falls to −40°C.

The nomadic Mongol tribes developed an intense and symbiotic relationship with their herds of horses, which provided them with their every need. Horse meat was food, the long tails and manes of these animals could be woven into ropes, their skin could be used to reinforce the felt of the tent-like *ger* against the piercing cold wind, their dung provided fuel. And their mares provided milk. Boiled and dried into chunks, this could be stored and carried. Fermented it provided acidic-tasting alcoholic *kumis*. Productive mares could be milked up to six times a day. And in times of extremity, especially when engaged in warfare, the tribesmen learned to slit a vein in their horse's neck, providing a small cup of blood, which would keep them alive.

Though the horses roamed free, they were trained to respond to their master's call, or whistle, like dogs. When the tribesmen were pursuing an enemy, they would bring along anything up to half a dozen horses each, so that they always had a fresh mount. Although the horses only weighed around 500 lbs, they could carry loads well in excess of their bodyweight. When ridden, they could gallop over six miles without a break. In the frigid cold of a winter's night, a Mongol would snuggle up against his horse for warmth. When they reached water, the rider would kneel down beside his mount to drink. Yet although a Mongol tribesman could always distinguish each of his collection of horses by its skin markings, he never gave them names. It was almost as if his horses were part of him, and needed no alien designation.

As the population on the steppe multiplied, the various

Mongol tribes began to fight over territory. These tough, warlike people, with their pony-sized steeds, soon became fearsome warriors. The saddles on which they rode had short stirrups, so that the rider could guide his horse with his legs, enabling him to use his arms to fire lethal metal-tipped arrows from his short bow with great accuracy. Tied to the saddle behind him was an array of weapons, which might include a scimitar, daggers, and a mace or a hatchet, as well as a leather bottle of milk. For armour, he wore cured horse-skin studded with metal.

Over the centuries a body of strict rules grew up concerning the treatment of horses, and woe betide any who broke them. This was exemplified in Genghis Khan's order: 'Seize and beat any man who breaks them . . . Any man . . . who ignores this decree, cut off his head where he stands.'

The man we know as Genghis Khan was born in a remote north-east corner of the Mongolian plateau, where the Siberian winds blow in from the mountains to the north. According to a local legend, seemingly undiluted by later folklore, these Mongols originated from the forests on the slopes of the mountains when the Blue-Grey Wolf mated with the Beautiful Red Doe, who gave birth by the shore of a large lake to the first of the Mongols, Bataciqan. The large lake is assumed to be Lake Baikal, in modern-day Russia. Some time after this, Bataciqan's descendants left the forests for the steppe, where they settled along the Onon River.

The Mongols saw themselves as different from the neighbouring Tartar and Turkic tribesmen, claiming descent through the ancient Huns, who founded their first empire in the region during the third century. (Hun is the

Mongolian for 'human being'.) It was these Huns who in the fourth and fifth centuries migrated west across Asia and into Europe, where they dispersed the Germanic tribes, the Vandals and the Goths, causing the movement of peoples that brought down the Roman Empire and ushered in the so-called Dark Ages.

Life on the steppe was hard for the Mongols. The chill Siberian winds brought intermittent rainfall. This froze on the mountainside in winter, melting in summer to flow down into blue lakes which spilled into rivers, bringing water to the vast parched grasslands that stretched to the empty horizon. Sometimes there would be no rainfall for years on end, with the sky remaining like a vast blue dome over the landscape. The endless blue sky, which spread from horizon to horizon in all directions, was worshipped as the One True God by these people. It was He who brought the clouds bearing rain.

Modern climatologists have discovered that some time after the birth of Genghis Khan, climate change began to moderate the weather of the region for several decades. This brought warmer temperatures and more rainfall. As a result, there was a widespread increase in grass. Herds of horses and other livestock were able to multiply, as did the tribesmen. The inevitable result was increasing tension between the nomadic tribesmen over large expanses of coveted land with no natural barriers. Without warning, tribesmen attacked the isolated *ger* of rival tribes, carrying off young women and boys into slavery. Outnumbered, the menfolk fled, carrying off their finest horses and wives in order to warn their allies, so that they could return to fight another day. Revenge was a constant driving force.

Into this world in 1162 was born a child named Temujin

(who would only later assume the name Genghis Khan). Temujin was the son of Yesugei, a leader of the important Borjigin clan, which lived close to the site of modern Ulaanbaatar. Temujin's early life was hard and brutal. When he was just nine, his father was poisoned, and his tribe cast out his mother Hoelun and all the family children. The oldest of these was Bekter, who was not directly related to any of them, being a son from Hoelun's murdered husband's previous marriage. Forced to scavenge for a living on the barren steppe, the close-knit family group hunted and foraged to stay alive, catching fish in the Onon River before it froze over for the winter.

An intense rivalry grew up between Bekter and Temujin, which came to a head when Temujin learned that Bektar intended to take Hoelun as his wife. Whereupon, Temujin stalked Bekter and slew him with an arrow. Bekter's last words to his brother are said to have been: 'Now you have no companion other than your shadow.' As far as can be gathered, Temujin was probably not yet even a teenager.

At this point it is worth pausing to examine how we have come to know these events in such detail. The story of Genghis Khan's life is recorded at some length in *The Secret History of the Mongols*, the bible of the Mongol people. This was written in the vertical lines of original Mongol script by an anonymous scribe some years after Temujin's death. *The Secret History of the Mongols* remained unknown to the West until a Chinese version was discovered by the nineteenth-century Russian monk, Pyotor Kafarov, during his travels in China. However, a faithful translation from the reconstructed Mongol text would not be made until as late as 1941 by the German sinologist, Erich Haenisch.

The work's flavour is biblical, and the accuracy of its text is of a similar order. In other words, it remains sacred to its people; yet apart from its mythological opening, it would seem to be a quasi-accurate narrative, this being confirmed by contemporary hearsay accounts passed down in stories.

The ancient Mongol language would remain purely verbal until Genghis Khan ordered the adoption of the script used by the Uighur Turks. These were the occupants of the large Xinjiang region of north-west China, which lies to the west of modern Mongolia, separated by the Gobi Desert. In the original Uighur script, and its Mongol variant, the letters of each word are written from top to bottom, i.e. vertically, in lines of words. These complete lines are then read in sequence from left to right.

The anonymous author of *The Secret History of the Mongols* indicates that it was finished in 'The Year of the Mouse'. The Mongols copied the Chinese calendar, which is based on a twelve-year cycle, with each year named after a different animal. Scholars scrutinising the events mentioned in the text have come to the conclusion that *The Secret History* was written in 1228, 1240 or perhaps even 1252.

We can now return to the adolescent fratricide, Temujin. When he arrived back at the family encampment, he encountered his mother Hoelun. With a mother's acumen, she realised at once what he had done. Immediately she flew into a rage, screaming at her son the very same words that the dying Bekter had uttered to him: 'Now you have no companion other than your shadow.' The psychology bred in Temujin by the simplicity and savagery of this almost primeval world can barely be imagined. Europe may have been a thousand miles distant, but it might as well have been a thousand years away.

On the other side of the world, Western civilisation had begun to stir once more, with a mature medieval culture beginning to emerge. Great gothic cathedrals were being built at Reims and Chartres, universities were already well established at places such as Oxford, Bologna and Paris. Meanwhile in the Arab Empire, amidst great cities such as Baghdad and Cordoba, the mosques and bazaars were thronged with populations numbering in the hundreds of thousands. And to the south of Mongolia, in nearby China, behind the protection of the Great Wall, the Jin dynasty under the Emperor Shizong was entering a period of peace and prosperity. This was a time of scholars and poets, wood blocks printing the texts of Confucius, and artists painting the birds and landscapes of the Chinese countryside.

Meanwhile in 1177, when Temujin was fifteen, he was taken captive by marauding tribesmen, who led him off to slavery in a cangue. This consisted of two large, heavy flat pieces of wood, carved so that they could be clapped closed around the prisoner's neck; the weight of the wood was a painful burden, and its size meant the prisoner was unable to feed himself with his hands, leaving him utterly dependent on his master. Miraculously, Temujin managed to persuade one of the tribesmen to help him escape. During this, and his consequent adventures, Temujin appears to have exhibited a winning charisma, inducing people to help him, and then to join up with him.

Prior to the death of Temujin's father, he had arranged for his son to be betrothed to a girl called Börte, in order to form an alliance with another powerful Mongol clan. Temujin now travelled to the Onggirat tribe to claim his bride. No sooner had he married Börte than she was kidnapped by neighbouring tribesmen. Temujin immediately led a campaign to avenge this crime, and soon retook his wife. Tales of Temujin's escape from slavery, and his bold rescue of Börte, earned him a high reputation for bravery and leadership. He soon rose up the tribal hierarchy, becoming a tribal chief.

By means of tactical alliances and tribal warfare, Temujin eventually established himself as leader of all the Mongol tribes. By 1206 he had become ruler of all the neighbouring tribes, including the Turkic Tatars and Uighurs. A gathering of the tribes – a *khuriltai* – was held, and Temujin was acknowledged as 'Genghis Khan' ('leader of all the people living in felt tents'). This unprepossessing title would soon strike fear into the hearts of all who heard it.

Genghis Khan was now undisputed ruler of the entire plateau 'from the Gobi [desert] in the south to the Arctic tundra in the north, from the Manchurian forests in the east to the Altai Mountains of the west'. Realising that this Mongol alliance would soon fall apart if it was not united and put to some use, in 1209 Genghis Khan launched a series of raids into nearby foreign territories. In 1211, spurred on by the sheer exultation of victory, Genghis Khan and his burgeoning army of horsemen rode south into northern China. The success of his furious but disciplined primitive army was beyond belief. Within the next few years, Genghis Khan had overthrown the Jin Dynasty. As he later explained: Heaven had grown weary of the excessive pride and luxury of the Chinese.

I am from the barbaric north. I wear the same clothing and eat the same food as the cow-herds and horse-herders.

We make the same sacrifice and share the same riches. I look upon the nation as a newborn child and I care for my soldiers as if they were my sons.

Prior to this, Genghis Khan went on, he had merely been interested in plunder. But now he had ridden south and succeeded in something that no one else had ever achieved in history. He had defeated the Chinese. And from them his army had learned how to use siege engines, catapults and even gunpowder. Genghis Khan now turned his eyes to the west and prepared to launch an attack upon kingdoms and empires, with long histories and fabled cities the like of which neither he nor his men had even dreamt existed. From now on, he vowed, he would unite the whole world in one empire.

Which brings us to the question of sideways history. Normally history is conceived as running in a linear trajectory. This may be seen as a vertical time-line on a graph. Sideways history may be seen as a horizontal line, taking account of various stages of history running in parallel. This is best illustrated by the twentieth-century economist, Milton Friedman, who observed that when he was living in San Francisco, he found himself living amidst almost the entire history of economics in its various stages of development. Around him he saw a great variety of immigrant communities and different classes: Chinatown, the Italian district, and many other social groups, each making use of their own cultural form of economic life. There was barter economy, credit economy, deferred debt economy, capital economy, and even the simple quasi-socialist communal economy practised by religious communities. Economics, in all its history, was alive and thriving around him.

Much the same can be said of the empires and countries occupying the Eurasian landmass in the early thirteenth century. In the east there was the highly stratified Chinese Empire. From the Near East to Spain was the Abbasid Caliphate, an essentially religious society, which still tolerated a degree of secular thinking in the form of science and philosophy. In Russia and Eastern Europe, tyrannies of primitive serfdom flourished. Meanwhile in Western Europe a variety of social administrations had sprung up. These ranged from democracy (Florence) to absolute monarchy (France), along with oligarchy (Venice); whilst in England there was a kingdom on the verge of the Magna Carta, which would grant citizens inalienable rights.

Almost all of these societies were evolving – more or less slowly – as they sought to absorb the political, social, economic and scientific advances that were stirring into life. Progress and survival would soon be the order of the day. All this begs a number of basic questions. What precisely *is* social progress? Who should benefit from it? And what is its aim? Indeed, does it even have an ultimate end: a utopia? These difficult questions remain without a final answer to this day, when it appears that liberal social democracy and economic advance are far from being the inevitable course of future civilisation.

Such questions will begin to arise of their own accord as we examine the empires that come into being in more progressive times. And as we shall see, any attempt to find even a provisional answer to them is not easy. Such questions continue to nag at our empire-building impulse.

However, it would seem that one thing can be stated for certain: the spread of the Mongol Empire across Eurasia did not result in what anyone would see as progress.

Or did it? History moves in mysterious ways, its blunders to perform. Despite the massive destruction involved in the Mongol invasion, some have seen this 'clearing of the ground' as a necessary prelude, sweeping away the social, political and cultural rigidities, which prepared the way for the more adaptable, more progressive civilisation to come. But first we must see what this freeing up of history involved.

In 1211 the Mongol invasion, led by Genghis Khan, swept westwards like fire burning through a map, and with similar results. They rode for thousands of miles through southern Siberia, across the Turkic lands, and then on to the Khwarazmian Empire. This empire of five million people occupied greater Persia and western Afghanistan, as far north as the Aral Sea. Its territory included historic cities such as Samarkand and Bukhara, which had grown rich from the Silk Route trade between China and Europe. Yet this large and sophisticated empire fell within two years to Genghis Khan's army.

How on earth did Genghis Khan and his army of primitive horsemen achieve all this, and with such speed? There was no doubting the efficiency and ferocity of his fighting men, organised in *tumen* – units of 10,000 men galloping behind their black horsehair *tug* banner. But how did Genghis Khan manage to instil discipline amongst such fiercely independent horsemen? How did he make them follow his pre-arranged tactics and commands?

The life of the Chinese military theoretician Sun Tzu, who wrote *The Art of War* around 500 BC, offers a clue here. Sun Tzu was ordered to appear before his leader, who had read his book and wished to test its author's theory on how to manage soldiers. Could it even be applied to women, for instance? Of course, replied Sun Tzu. Whereupon he divided the leader's 180 concubines into two companies, each armed with spears, selecting a leader for each company. He then attempted to drill the two groups, passing on orders to their leaders. But all of the young women simply burst out laughing.

Sun Tzu explained to his leader: 'If words of command are not clear and thoroughly understood, then the general is to blame.' He ordered the leader of each group to be beheaded, replacing them with a different leader. When the next orders were given to the leaders and passed on to the two groups, both groups carried out their orders with alacrity and great efficiency. Although Genghis Khan certainly never read Sun Tzu, his method of instilling discipline amongst his men was remarkably similar.[18]

As for the rest, Genghis Khan knew the speed, endurance and ruthlessness of his horsemen, and employed his lightning tactics accordingly. A typical move was for him to use heavy firepower to blast a passage through the enemy lines for his cavalry units, which were then deployed with maximum efficiency, piercing the enemy line and then fanning out behind their rear, cutting their supply lines and instilling panic, which caused the enemy to flee in all directions. Communication between separate units was

---

18 Such ruthlessness is not confined to the distant past. The twentieth-century Soviet leader Joseph Stalin, no more an aficionado of military self-help manuals than Genghis Khan, adopted an uncannily similar policy to that recommended by Sun Tzu. During his 1930s Great Purge and indeed well into the Second World War, Stalin ordered the execution of literally hundreds of his military leaders (over 80 per cent of his commanders in the majority of sectors were purged), with a similar salutary effect on their successors and the men they commanded.

maintained by the use of flags. Indeed, it is to the Mongols that we owe the art of semaphore.

The lasting effect of these tactics can be seen in the fact that the German Second World War Panzer General, Heinz Guderian, the master of Blitzkrieg, identified the inspiration of his tactics as Genghis Khan. Though the ruthlessness with which Genghis Khan followed through on his tactics is another matter. According to Khan's biographer Jack Weatherford: 'The objective of such tactics was simple and always the same: to frighten the enemy into surrendering before an actual battle began.' Any who then resisted could expect the very worst. After taking Samarkand, Genghis Khan ordered the entire population to be assembled in the plain outside the city walls. Here they were systematically butchered, their severed heads arranged in pyramids.

In Bukhara, as his Mongol soldiers burnt the city to the ground, Genghis Khan addressed the wailing remnant population in the main mosque, announcing that he was the 'flail of God' sent to punish them for their sins. When the Khan's Mongol army took Gurganj, the capital of the Khwarazmian Empire, the thirteenth-century Persian scholar, Juvayni, recorded that Genghis Khan's 50,000 Mongol soldiers were commanded by their leader to kill twenty-four citizens each. As there were not enough citizens to meet this command, and the soldiers well understood the punishment for not fulfilling their leader's orders to the letter, the ensuing swift and competitive slaughter of several hundred thousand people resulted in what has been called 'the bloodiest massacre in human history'.

An enigmatic, somewhat bland portrait of Genghis Khan in his later years conveys little of the sheer terror his presence could inspire. It was drawn around forty-five years after his death, but the artist consulted with men who had known Genghis Khan closely during his lifetime. Originally black and white, it was softened by colour during the following century.

Genghis Khan.

Genghis Khan now returned to Mongolia, but despatched two of his most trusted generals, Chepe and Subutai, north with 20,000 horsemen. This army swept up through the Caucasus and into Russia. Here they were confronted by an army of 80,000 men, which they annihilated. Instead of occupying this territory, they then withdrew: Genghis Khan had ordered that this was to be merely a 'reconnaissance mission'.

Such exemplary slaughter brings us to the deeper problem of morality, and questions concerning the ethics of conquest and empire. Indeed, is there any such thing as morality involved in the imperial enterprise? The usual justification for such conquest is the spreading of progressive civilisation. Beneath this lie even more fundamental questions concerning the ethics of empire, and the morality of progressive civilisation itself. Is there such a thing as either? And if so, why should we regard such things as universal? Are all human beings equal? Should they all be treated in the same fashion? Should they all be subjected to the same universal laws? If so, what is the ultimate moral law?

Over the centuries, and over its extensive reach and influence, the Western tradition has come up with surprisingly similar answers. The biblical Book of Leviticus, written around 1400 BC, stated: 'Love your neighbour as yourself.' (Freud would declare this: 'The commandment which is impossible to fulfil.') Despite this, similar injunctions would appear in Buddhism, Taoism, Hinduism, and indeed most of the world's major religions. One and a half millennia after Leviticus, Jesus Christ would exhort his followers: 'Do unto others as you would have them do unto you.' Six centuries later, Muhammad would pronounce: 'As you would have people do to you, do to them.'

Over a millennium after this, Europe's leading philosopher, Emmanuel Kant, would recognise that such an injunction did not necessarily involve a belief in God. Yet his analysis of ethics led him to a remarkably similar conclusion to all those previous theisms, when he declared the fundamental principle of morality to be: 'Treat others as you would wish to be treated.' It would take another 300 years before modern thinkers recognised that such a sentiment was inadequate. As Freud understood, it is psychologically impossible to maintain such a stance on a permanent basis. This was simply not how we actually lived or behaved in a social setting: our moral thinking did not work like this.

The Lebanese-American thinker, Nassim Taleb, has transmogrified this basic principle of morality into a maxim that more closely reflects our moral needs, ethical thinking and behaviour: 'Do not to others what you don't want them to do to you.' The inapposite double negative may make it less easily comprehensible. (Is it simply a sleight of hand reversal, or turning inside out, of the Leviticus-Christ-Kant maxim? Examine it carefully: it is not.)[19] This would seem closer to a basic instruction for the guidance of our actual moral behaviour. Not so much love thy neighbour, as proceed with due care . . .

It is not difficult to see Genghis Khan adhering to this maxim. For a boy whose father had been murdered, whose step-brother had plotted to marry his mother, and who had been taken into slavery, enduring the pain and humiliation of the cangue, he can have been under few illusions about what others wanted to do to him. And he had certainly chosen to act accordingly, pyramids of skulls and all. In fact, the question of morality and empire remains open, leaving us with little but clichés. Might is right; history

---

19 Muhammad himself declared in the Hadith: 'What you dislike to be done to you, don't do to them.' However, in the ensuing century of the Muslim conquest, this evidently fell into abeyance.

is written by the victors; and so forth. Only the hindsight of historians begins to add any perspective to such views. But this comes later. Where empires are concerned, the certainty of the present often prevails with much the same conviction as that held by Genghis Khan.

Genghis Khan would die at the age of sixty-five in 1227, ironically from injuries sustained from falling off his horse while crossing the Gobi Desert. Genghis Khan's grave has yet to be found. According to legend, a river was diverted over his burial place, so that it would never be discovered. Such a ritual harks back to the beginnings of historical time: both Gilgamesh and Attila the Hun are said to have been buried in the same way.

Even before Genghis Khan's death, a *khuriltai* had been called to decide who amongst his sons should be his successor. This had broken up in acrimony. Following his death, the empire was divided into several khanates governed by his sons. However, his third son, Ögedei, would eventually be recognised as the second 'Great Khan' of the Mongol Empire.

Ögedei was renowned for his love of alcohol, and on his installation as Khan he became so drunk that he 'threw open his father's treasury and riotously distributed all the riches stored there'.

Despite such an inauspicious start, Ögedei would prove a more than competent ruler. He was not inclined to lead the Mongol armies on campaigns and preferred to remain in his capital Karakorum, overseeing the campaigns and organising the administration. The gathering of taxes throughout the empire was modelled on the Chinese system, with the monies being collected by local 'tax farmers'. Likewise, paper money was circulated, backed by silver. (At the time, paper itself remained a novelty in Europe, let alone paper money.)

The problem of communications throughout the vast empire had already been solved by Genghis Khan, who instituted a network of relay stations. As the Mongol army moved at speed, its communications system had to be even faster. Messengers riding on relays of horses could cover more than 150 miles a day over almost any terrain. (Such speeds and efficiency would not be matched for over 600 years, until the advent of the Trans-American Pony Express.)

Although Ögedei did not lead his men into battle, the empire continued to expand under his reign, pushing far into Europe. In 1241, the Mongols won the Battle of Legnica in Poland, and western Europe lay at their feet. News then spread throughout the empire of Ögedei's death, and the commanders rode back as fast as they could to take part in the *khuriltai* to elect a new leader. By such chance was Europe saved from a Mongol invasion.

An uncannily similar situation would arise in 1258, after the Mongols had overrun the Abbasid capital, Baghdad. Egypt and the remnants of the entire Abbasid Empire lay at their feet. Then news came through that the fourth Great Khan, Möngke Khan, had died, and the leaders once more galloped off east for the *khuriltai*, leaving behind an ill-organised Mongol army. In 1260 this was defeated in Palestine by the Mamlukes at the Battle of Ain Jalut. Egypt, North Africa and Al-Andalus were spared the Mongol onslaught.

In that same year, Kublai Khan became the fifth Great Khan of the Mongol Empire. During his reign, the empire definitively split into four separate khanates. Instead of attempting to reunite the empire, Kublai Khan turned his attentions south to China, moving his capital to Khanbaliq (Beijing), with the intention of forming an entirely new empire.

Sequence

The three khanates to the west of Kublai Khan's realm were the Golden Horde (occupying the territory north of the Black Sea and the Caspian, extending north and east into what is now Russia and Kazakhstan), the Chagatai Khanate (Afghanistan and north-east central Asia south of the Golden Horde), and the Ilkhanate (Greater Persia and west into Anatolia). All of these would convert to Islam (hence Il-Khanate), while Kublai Khan's realm adopted Buddhism. The Golden Horde would eventually give way to Russia, but not before it had dealt a blow which turned the course of European history.

In 1348, Mongols of the Golden Horde were besieging the Crimean city of Kaffa (modern Feodosia), which was then a Black Sea trading port of the Genoese. When there was an outbreak of bubonic plague in the Mongol army, they catapulted plague-ridden corpses over the walls. (Some claim this as the earliest example of germ warfare.) Consequently, ships sailing from Kaffa to Europe transported the plague to Italy. Within half a dozen years, the Black Death (as it came to be known) had spread across Europe from Lisbon to Novgorod, from Sicily to Norway, in the process killing between 30 to 60 per cent of the entire population, probably accounting for over 100 million deaths.

A proto-Renaissance of European culture, inspired by a variety of disparate sources such as the Sicilian court of Frederick the Great ('Stupor Mundi'), scientific and philosophical ideas imported from the Muslim world, and the new naturalistic painting of the Italian Giotto, was halted in its tracks, delaying the actual Italian Renaissance by a century.

5

The Yuan Dynasty

Kublai Khan proclaimed the Yuan Dynasty in 1271, and set about completing his conquest of the Sung Dynasty of southern China, which would eventually unite north and south China for the first time since the Sung Dynasty had split off from the Jin Dynasty almost 150 years previously. China has traditionally flourished during periods when the north and south have been united. Unification would always prove difficult over such a vast region, although the people occupying this region are, and have been throughout history, for the most part homogenous Han Chinese.[20]

Any consideration of Chinese history must be seen from the perspective of its long past, as well as the effect this may well have upon its future, and thus the future of world history. Effects and influences can take centuries to be understood. According to the story, when China's twentieth-century communist ruler, Chairman Mao, was asked in

---

20 The present-day population of China is classified as over 90 per cent Han Chinese, with minorities such as the Uighur, a Turkic Muslim people, Mongols and others, making up the remainder. However, such is the populousness of China that the Uighur population consists of more than 11 million people.

the 1960s about the impact of the French Revolution, he is said to have replied, 'It is too early to tell.'

Subsequent sources, hampered by a similar lack of hard facts, claim that this remark was really made by his prime minister, Zhou Enlai, who was said to have been referring to the Paris 1968 Student Revolution. The Chairman Mao version better illustrates the Chinese attitude towards historical effect. Even in Chinese communism, it is possible to detect age-old Buddhist influences which coloured attitudes back through the dynasties to the Yuan period and beyond.

Unlike the previous empires we have discussed, which had their own origin myths, the Yuan Dynasty (1271–1368) was born out of a succession of previous dynasties. By the time of its birth, Dynastic China was already a mature culture, with a recognisable quasi-continuous history. As previously mentioned, Chinese Han civilisation evolved independently in the Yellow River basin of central China around 2,000 BC, i.e. a millennium or so after the Mesopotamian and Nilotic civilisations. Out of this Han civilisation, the legendary first Xia dynasty is said to have developed. Han rule gradually spread by 'migration and assimilation', which included the process of 'sinicisation', the adoption of the same diet, writing, language, lifestyle and general culture of the Han.

The original dynasty of a united Imperial China was the Qin Dynasty, which began in 221 BC. This covered a territory recognisable as China, stretching from the borders of modern Manchuria as far south as modern Vietnam, and west towards Sichuan. Qin (pronounced 'Chin') is generally recognised as the origin of the name China. This dynasty is today remembered for its founding emperor, Qin Shi Huang, who died in 210 BC leaving behind him a terracotta army, whose purpose was to protect him in the afterlife. Surprisingly, this was only discovered by accident in 1974 by some local farmers digging a well, which penetrated a vast hollow underground mausoleum.

The making of Qin Shi Huang's mausoleum is a feat in many ways comparable to the construction of the sphinx and the pyramids. His 'army' consisted of over 8,000 soldiers (all with individualised features), 130 chariots and 670 horses. Its construction, along with the mausoleum itself, hidden beneath a hill-sized mound, is thought to have involved 700,000 men, drawn from all over the empire. According to Sima Qian, the father of Chinese history, writing in the ensuing century:

> The First Emperor was buried with palaces, towers, officials, valuable artefacts and wondrous objects . . . 100 flowing rivers were simulated using mercury, and above them the ceiling was decorated with heavenly bodies below which were the features of the land.

For more than two millennia this was regarded as fantasy, or at best legend. And even after the discovery of Qin Shi Huang's mausoleum, certain features of Sima Qian's description were taken as fanciful embellishments. However, consequent archaeological investigations have revealed high levels of mercury in the soil that once obscured the mausoleum, raising all manner of questions regarding any 'palaces, towers . . . valuable artefacts and wondrous objects' yet to be discovered. Curiously, Qian's original manuscript makes no reference to any terracotta army, suggesting that possibly the very existence of this unprecedented collection remained a secret from the outset, with its creators being put to death.

This too is not so far-fetched as it sounds. The other great construction dating from Emperor Qin's reign was an early crude version of the Great Wall of China, made of locally gathered stones and compacted earth. The precise length of this wall remains unknown, as most of it has either been eroded away over the centuries or become incorporated into the present structure. Even so, it is known to have covered more than 3,000 miles.[21]

This certainly gives an indication of how the Chinese viewed the threat from the nomadic tribesmen who occupied the vast plateau to the north. (The Mongols would not emerge as the dominant tribe for almost another one and a half millennia.) Even more suggestive of this Chinese fear is the sheer cost of Qin's wall. This was no great work of art, such as his intricate and wondrous mausoleum – yet where human life was concerned, the cost was if anything even greater. According to some modern historians: 'it has been estimated . . . that hundreds of thousands, if not up to a million, workers died building the Qin wall.'

Yet this vast expenditure of human life would be followed by the laying of the foundations of a civilisation that would, in the centuries to come, grow to equal and then excel any other civilisation on earth. It is no exaggeration to say that the Qin Dynasty created the social blueprint for most of the great dynasties to come over the ensuing two millennia (or longer, as we shall see some now argue). And how did the Qin Dynasty achieve this feat – which would in time produce an empire, in the form of the Yuan Dynasty, that was greater and more civilised

---

21 i.e. considerably more than the distance between Los Angeles and Miami, or the length of the Roman Empire.

than that of Rome, more artistically and technologically creative than the Caliphates?

It was the Qin Dynasty that instigated a centralised government and employed a vast civil service of scholar-officials who administered throughout the empire. This latter fact is, and remains, vital to the understanding of Chinese culture. Such a far-flung administration involved government by individual officials, rather than rule according to an established legal code. What could be termed criminal or rebellious behaviour was dealt with by penal sanctions. Yet without a universal code of law, what guided these scholar-officials in their administration of justice?

It is here that we see the pervasive influence of Confucius. Not for nothing have his teachings been characterised as the 'philosophy of civil servants'. Confucius had died some three centuries previously, but by now his teachings had become much more than a philosophy or a religion. *The Analects of Confucius*, a collection of his sayings painstakingly assembled after his death by his followers, was by now widely circulated. Indeed, they had become a spiritual-ethical guidance that embodied an entire way of life.

Membership of the civil service was dependent upon a deep and rigorous knowledge of Confucian teachings. Entrance exams were particularly gruelling, with candidates locked in tiny cells containing just a writing board and a bucket, for anything up to three days. This was designed to weed out members of well-connected families, relatives of previous civil servants, and such. It ensured that entry was entirely a matter of merit. The Qin Dynasty would last for only fifteen years, making it by far the shortest of the great Chinese dynasties, yet it 'inaugurated an imperial system that lasted, with interruption and adaptation, until

1912': the year when the last emperor abdicated and the Republic of China was established.[22]

So what are the teachings of Confucius, which so moulded the Chinese character? His ultimate aim was the achievement of harmony, in both the personal and civil spheres. On the personal level: 'When one cultivates to the utmost the principles of his nature, and exercises them on the principle of reciprocity, he is not far from the path.' Adding, in evidence of his understanding of how we actually behave, the all too recognisable: 'What you do not like when done to yourself, do not to others.'

Yet, as with so many, he found himself forced to disregard such sentiment when it came to the practical business of administration, which is of course the imposition of power, wanted or unwanted, no matter how it is disguised. The pious Confucius commends: 'He who exercises government by means of his virtue remains as steadfast as the north star in the sky.' The more practical Confucius commends: 'Pay strict attention to business, be true to your word, be economical in expenditure, and love your people.'

Buddhism, with its message of compassion and lack of attachment to this world, would arrive in China in the century following the Qin Dynasty. Initially, Confucianism abhorred its nihilistic approach, but Buddhism would eventually strike a deep chord in the Chinese national character. By the advent of the Yuan Dynasty, it had become the official religion. The reason for Buddhism's deep accord with the Chinese is not difficult to discern. The almost casual mass destruction of human life, as noted in the Qin

---

22 Only Judaism can claim a longer continuity; only the intermittent tradition of democracy matches its philosophical longevity.

Dynasty for instance, would invariably be followed by a cultural resurgence, which even so contained the seeds of its own destruction. This ever-revolving wheel of fortune led to widespread uncertainties, which naturally fostered the withdrawal from worldly ambitions advocated by Buddhism.

Such cycles have been a recurrent feature of Chinese history. The two most recent examples are perhaps the most instructive. The fighting before, during and after the Second World War, lasted from 1937 to 1949 in this part of Asia. During this period China was ravaged by Japanese invasion and then civil war, both involving mass slaughter amongst the civilian population, as well as the military participants. Such was the brutality and chaos that estimates of over fifteen million Chinese deaths are usually accepted.

Yet within decades, under the communist dictatorship of the charismatic Chairman Mao Zedong, this ravaged land embarked upon the 'Great Leap Forward'. This would 'transform agricultural production, using people's communes to walk the road from socialism to communism, from poverty to abundance'. In the process China would become a world superpower, capable of resisting the combined force of the Western Powers in the Korean War, even vying with the Soviet Union for the leadership of world communism.

The fact that all this contained the seeds of its own destruction came to be seen in Chairman Mao's decision to launch the Cultural Revolution in 1966, intended to mobilise the people once more and return to the basics of 'ideological purity'. Mao's *Little Red Book* of quotations took on the role of Confucius's Analects, and a wave of destruction was launched throughout the land. How many died during these upheavals? 'Nobody knows, because nobody counted.' Consequent estimates suggest that over three million people died, and 100 million people (a ninth of the population) were uprooted and displaced during this agony of self-destruction and famine, which would plague China for a decade.

Yet within forty years this devastated country had made the greatest 'leap forward' ever witnessed in human history, building the architectural wonder of the world in the form of the Shanghai waterfront, sending a rocket to the moon, and becoming the world's second largest economy. All this, without the liberal social democracy and free market that was deemed essential to rapid economic growth. Whether this too contains the seeds of its own destruction – as authoritarianism of dynastic proportions coexists uneasily with a release of social mobility, energy and creativity never previously witnessed on such a scale – remains to be seen.

All of which places us in a suitable context to begin examining in detail the Yuan Dynasty, otherwise known as the Great Yuan. And why is this so? Perhaps most pertinently, the Yuan Dynasty stands in a pivotal mid-way position between the founding Qin Dynasty, and what for want of a better name might be called the Post-Mao Dynasty. At a certain point in all three of these dynasties, it could be claimed that China stood poised to lead the world. Only during the Yuan Dynasty has it actually achieved this feat.

When Kublai Khan finally completed his conquest of the Sung Dynasty in 1279, he did not follow the example of his grandfather, Genghis Khan. During the long and arduous campaign that preceded this victory, the Mongol army was not unleashed in its traditional orgy of destruction, with populations put to the sword, cities left in smoking

ruins and pyramids of skulls. Kublai Khan set about sini-
cising himself and his rule. The capital was established in
Khanbaliq (Beijing), and he graciously invited the Song
Empress Dowager and her eight-year-old grandson,
Emperor Gong of Song, to take up residence in the city
under his protection.

At the same time, Kublai Khan embarked upon a policy
of further expansion, now reaching beyond China in pursuit
of a pan-Asiatic empire. Korea and Manchuria soon fell.
Invasions were launched against North Vietnam and the
southern Vietnamese kingdom of Champa, as well as Thai
territory and Burma. To the north, his navy attacked the
large island territory of Sakhalin off the east coast of Siberia.
None of these territories was completely conquered, but
most were forced to concede vassal status to Yuan China.

However, despite repeated attempts to invade Japan –
one with a fleet of almost 1,000 ships – weather, faulty
ship construction, and fierce Samurai resistance, along with
inaccurate maps, all combined to thwart Kublai Khan's
ambitions. Another invasion of far-flung Java proved similarly unsuccessful, once again frustrated by bad maps.

Other cartographic enterprises proved more successful.
The countries along the Silk Road were accurately mapped,
with the aid of expert Islamic geographers. Similarly, the
renowned Kangnido 'map of the world', which dates from
before Admiral Zheng He set out on his great voyages,
indicates that Yuan Dynasty geographers were well aware
of the existence of India, Arabia and Africa – if a little
uncertain about their actual shape and size.

The Mongols and their emperor, Kublai Khan, may
have conquered China, but the extensive territory of which
they took possession and ruled contained a far more

advanced civilisation than that of the Mongols. Indeed, Kublai Khan's first great contribution to this civilisation was simply not destroying it. Inevitably, the years of war against the Song Dynasty had resulted in widespread destruction. Indeed, the city on the site of what would become Khanbaliq had been reduced to ruins. But as part of his sinicisation process, Kublai Khan ordered a new capital to be built in the Chinese style. Initially, he and his Mongol commanders for the most part presided over their new possession, but as the years passed, the new Yuan emperor would make his own distinct contribution.

When Marco Polo arrived at Kublai Khan's palace in Khanbaliq around 1275, several years into the new emperor's reign, he found 'the greatest palace that ever was . . . The hall of the palace is so large that it can easily accommodate 6,000 people.' The city itself was enclosed by walls six miles long by six miles wide. This was one of the termini of the Silk Road, and the city had separate quarters for foreign merchants of different religions. These included Nestorians (Christians of a heretical sect long since banished from Europe), Jews, 'Saracans' (Muslims) and even Manicheans (a Persian dualistic religion that briefly rivalled Christianity during Roman times, which the Chinese classified as 'vegetarian demon-worshippers').

As this indicates, the Silk Road was responsible for the dissemination of ideas as well as trade, and it was around this period that the ideas of the Islamic philosopher-scientists began arriving in China, promulgating Aristotelian philosophy and Greek medicine. Chinese Muslim physicians became responsible for the establishment of hospitals, and Khanbaliq became known as 'the Department for Extensive Mercy'.

Kublai Khan's greatest domestic contribution was the dredging and reopening of China's ancient Grand Canal, which led to a resurgence of the Chinese economy. Parts of this canal dated back as far as 500 BC, but it had not become linked up along its entire 1,000-mile length until a millennium later, before falling into disrepair during the ensuing centuries. This amazing feat of engineering remains to this day the oldest and longest artificial inland waterway in the world. When Kublai Khan reopened the canal, it stretched from Khanbaliq through the Eastern Chinese hinterland all the way to the city of Hangzhou, which 300 years earlier had been the capital of China.

When Marco Polo arrived at Hangzhou, 'the city of heaven', he could hardly believe his eyes. This was:

> The finest and most splendid city in all the world, filled with wide and spacious waterways. On one side of the city is a lake of crystal-clear fresh water. Its shores are thirty miles long and filled with stately palaces and mansions of such splendour that it is impossible to imagine anything more beautiful. These are the abodes of nobles and magnates. At the same time there are also cathedrals and monasteries. The surface of the lake is covered with all manner of barges filled with pleasure-seekers . . .

No such city existed in Europe, or anywhere else in the world. Even Venice appeared but a pale miniature imitation. Once again, we come to the concept of sideways history, with separate regions simultaneously at different stages of historical development. In the remnant of the caliphates, Al-Andalus, the mixture of religions and learning had provided a ferment of ideas, with superb architecture such as the Grand Mosque in Cordoba and the Alhambra Gardens in Granada; but all this stood in peril from the southward advance of the Christian armies through the Iberian peninsula.

Meanwhile in the heart of Europe, the Dark Ages had long since given way to a revival of education, with great centres of learning such as the Sorbonne in Paris attracting students from far and wide, as well as a resurgence of architecture with teams of skilled artisans and stonemasons erecting gothic cathedrals in the heart of cities throughout the continent. Yet none of this compared with the splendours of Hangzhou.[23]

In Roman times, Europe had led the world; during the caliphates the Middle East had seen the most advanced civilisation; and now China was beginning to emerge as the world leader. But here was something utterly new. Europe and the Middle East had cross-fertilised ideas and technologies, borrowing from each other as their ships traded across the Mediterranean. China, on the other hand, was largely *sui generis*, developing its own ideas in isolation

---

23 It is worth emphasising here that modern sideways history is far from being confined to Milton Friedman's San Francisco. It can be experienced by anyone who ventures beyond the confines of a twenty-first-century tropical beach resort into the previous centuries of its developing world surroundings.

Furthermore, some years ago I witnessed on TV one of the most extreme and poignant examples of sideways history. An astronomer, of Native American lineage, was working at an observatory in New Mexico. After demonstrating his telescope and its ability to detect stars billions of light-years away, he went outside onto the open-air platform. Away in the night he pointed out the fires of a Native American reservation, where they were still enacting their prehistoric rituals. 'That is where I come from.'

and retaining its secrets. Illustrative of this is the Silk Road, which was already well developed by the time it was described by Herodotus in the fifth century BC.

The *raison d'être* of this network of interlinked trade routes lies in its name. China had discovered how to produce silk, which became a valued luxury in the West. The manufacture of this product, which was spun by the silkworm in its chrysalis, remained a closely guarded secret. Not until the tenth century did two Nestorian monks manage to smuggle out silkworm eggs, concealed in the hollowed-out tops of their walking canes, enabling the secret to reach the West.

China was to come up with several fundamental discoveries that would remain secret, until knowledge of their manufacture seeped out to the West. In many, though not all cases, this would result in their further development, which would often change the face of world history. Paper was discovered, and the making of it developed in China, during the first and second centuries AD. It would be almost a millennium before this technique reached Europe. Similarly, gunpowder was discovered by the Chinese sometime around the turn of the first millennium AD. Its military use would soon be exploited in such weapons as 'fire arrows', the 'mother of a hundred bullets gun', and 'thunderclap bombs' (similar to stone grenades), whose shrapnel could inflict lethal wounds over a wide area.

Ironically, gunpowder had been discovered by Chinese alchemists searching for the elixir of life: the mythical substance that promised to preserve the life, and youth, of any who drank it. This was a persistent favourite of Chinese emperors. The first Qin emperor, Qin Shi Huang, is known to have died of 'elixir poisoning' in 210 BC.

Elixir ingredients prepared by later imperial alchemists included ground pearl, gold leaf and other precious substances known for their incorruptibility. More ambitious alchemists introduced mercury and salts of arsenic, which had the opposite of the desired effect. Chinese alchemists' search for an elixir of life would continue to lead the world until the eighteenth-century Qing Dynasty.

This knowledge too would spread to Europe, gaining credence amongst accomplished and susceptible physicians alike. Lorenzo the Magnificent, lying on his deathbed in fifteenth-century Florence, was administered an elixir containing ground pearl, which would later become a favourite of English Victorian physicians who catered for the wealthy. The dream of eternal life is a persistent fairy tale, which has occupied a permanent place in every great empire throughout all human history. It persists to this day in the form of cryogenics, in which a gullible plutocrat pays for his cadaver to be frozen to below -130°C, in the expectation that one day he will return to amaze his descendants.

But back to the unfortunately more realistic infliction of death. It would be several centuries before the formula for gunpowder reached Europe, where its potential was little realised, and it would be used mainly in the production of spectacular firework displays. It was the Mongol invasion of the Middle East and eastern Europe, and the widespread use of explosive fire arrows by their horsemen, which altered this perception. Witnessing this new weapon, some unremembered inventor made a simple connection of genius, and invented the cannon.

According to the twentieth-century Arab historian, Ahmad al-Hassan, the victorious Mamlukes used 'the first cannon in history' at the vital Battle of Ain Jalut, which halted the Mongols in 1260. This claim remains disputed, but what cannot be disputed is the transformative effect of the cannon on military history. From that time on, the days of castles, arrows, armour, cavalry even, and all manner of military hardware, were effectively numbered. With the advent of artillery, warfare would never be the same again.[24]

Not surprisingly, the Chinese also invented the cannon for themselves. In 1341, the historian Xian Zhang recorded that a cannonball fired from an 'eruptor [could] pierce the heart or belly when it strikes a man or horse, and can transfix several persons at once'. The list of cultural firsts invented, and fully developed, by the Yuan Dynasty continues to astonish. Most of these would trickle through to Europe, more or less slowly, usually by way of the Silk Road. Others would remain uniquely Chinese.

The most influential Yuan discoveries would transform Western civilisation, when they at last reached the outer world. As we have seen, paper had been invented some time previously, and the Song Dynasty had even experimented with paper money. However, it was the skilled administrators of the Yuan court who took this idea to its limit, with the introduction of a centralised system of paper currency. This could not only be printed by special wooden blocks at the Imperial Mint, but could also be used to control the economy. Never before had paper been used as the prevalent form of currency throughout the land.

Not only did these early Chinese financiers invent this

---

24 The military mind being such as it is, this fact would take centuries to sink in. It is no surprise that Napoleon learned his trade as a lowly artillery officer, and even half a century later, many would fail to recognise the Charge of the Light Brigade as a celebration of futility.

form of money, but they also understood how to use it. As we have seen, previous Chinese administrations had introduced various attempts at paper money backed by silver. But the Yuan paper currency – known as Chao – was a fiat currency. That is, it was backed by nothing but government regulation, which simply *said* that it was worth what it was. As such, it was what is now known as fiduciary money: reliant solely upon the confidence of those who used it.[25] This was no mean feat. The first attempt to introduce similar banknotes in Europe would come some 500 years later. In 1720, the Scots financier John Law would be placed in charge of the French treasury, and begin issuing paper money, an experiment that would end in disaster. (France would not accept paper currency for almost another century.)

The other great Yuan achievement was the establishment of the modern printing press. Various methods of printing had been known for some centuries previously in China, but it was a civil servant named Wang Zhen who definitively re-invented printing in 1298, with moveable wooden type containing the many characters of the Chinese alphabet. This enabled the establishment of printing presses that could mass produce entire books. Not until the following century would this method be established in Europe by Johannes Gutenberg. Precisely how much he knew about Chinese methods that had spread to the Middle East remains unclear.

Either way, this invention would revolutionise China,

---

25 All the world's currencies are now fiduciary money. Regular over-production of banknotes, resulting in inflation and spectacular collapses in value, remind us of the precariousness of such currency. It also shows the expertise with which these pioneer Yuan Dynasty financiers handled this new form of money that they had invented.

and then Europe, where it would be a catalyst for the Renaissance, spreading images, learning and new ideas. In Yuan China, it would bring about a transformation of culture and the arts that was uniquely oriental. Most notably this would include the development of a distinctive Chinese form of drama, the invention of the novel as a literary form, and the evolution of landscape painting as a form of poetic expression. A high point was the creation of 'The Three Perfections', a characteristically Chinese art form, which combined poetry, calligraphy and painting in a single work. However, the Yuan Dynasty's most exquisite creation was the development of a blue and white porcelain, which would never be surpassed.[26]

A Yuan Dynasty example of the Three Great Perfections:
poetry, calligraphy and painting.

---

26 Nowadays fine examples of Yuan blue and white porcelain can fetch in excess of £3 million, more even than the better-known Ming porcelain.

But it is perhaps in science that the Yuan dynasty excelled. It would be three centuries before Galileo crystalised the scientific revolution in Europe with his realisation that 'the universe is written in the language of mathematics'. Yet by this time Chinese scientists and mathematicians were already making discoveries that would have amazed their European contemporaries as much as Harun al-Rashid's ornate clock had astonished the court of Charlemagne in the Dark Ages. By 1290, the Yuan astronomer Guo Shoujing had completed a calendar that calculated the terrestrial year as 365.2425 days, i.e. within 26 seconds of its present measurement. He also solved a major hydrological difficulty in the completion of the Grand Canal, and invented a host of astronomical measuring devices, which would not be superseded until the invention of the telescope.

In the light of such achievements, it comes as little surprise that the thirteenth-century Yuan mathematician, Zhu Shijie, 'raised Chinese algebra to the highest level'. In particular, he devised a method for solving simultaneous equations with four unknowns, introduced matrix methods, as well as what we now know as Pascal triangles. Here again is a classic example of sideways history. These algebraic concepts would remain unknown in Europe until they were discovered independently some three centuries later. Chinese and European mathematics would continue to develop in parallel, yet unevenly and without contact, for many years to come.

Similar parallelism, of a more synchronous kind, can be seen in the development of the magnetic compass. The compass had been known in China since the Qin Dynasty, when it had been used for occult divination practices. Its elevation from quackery to maritime navigational use was a direct result of the Yuan scientific outlook. Meanwhile identical developments were taking place quite independently in Europe, enabling medieval sailors to venture directly across the Bay of Biscay, rather than hugging the coast. This was, of course, nothing compared to the truly astounding navigational journeys of Zheng He during the ensuing Ming Dynasty.

By the fourteenth century, the Yuan Dynasty was beginning to fall apart. In the end, its success in so many fields proved incompatible. Recall Marco Polo's description of the lakeside shore at Hangzhou, which was lined by no less than thirty miles of stately palaces and splendid mansions. Rapid economic progress had, as ever, led to excessive benefit for the upper strata of society, meanwhile the masses remained crippled by taxes. Class conflict became inevitable. Such troubles were exacerbated by a series of natural disasters. Three times the Yellow River burst its banks, leading to catastrophic floods, famine and loss of life.

The end came with a peasant uprising, which rapidly spread from province to province. The military too revolted, and in 1368 the capital fell and a new Han emperor was installed in place of the previous Mongol incumbent. The Ming Dynasty had begun.

This too would be one of the great dynasties, though not quite as formative as the Yuan Dynasty. And it too contained the seeds of its own disaster, which would transform China for centuries to come. The Confucian scholar-officials who had been so instrumental in creating such an efficient and coordinated imperial administration had now become hidebound with rigid traditions and creeping corruption. Such an institution did not take easily to the new challenges posed by scientific inventions and pioneering exploration by the likes of Admiral Zheng He. Such things did nothing but upset the personal and civil harmony required by Confucian teachings.

By the early decades of the fifteenth century, the administration had begun to prevail upon the emperor. China isolated itself from the outside world and the scientific revolution ground to a halt. The progressive society that had led the world began to ossify. Ming vases, exquisite poetry, art and opera reached perfection. Harmony had become absolute. And static.

Sequence

By now individual civilisations had begun to evolve at several new locations across the globe. These ranged from the Songhai Empire in West Africa to the Moghul Empire in India, as well as the Rus of Ivan the Terrible, which had emerged in the Duchy of Moscow after the expulsion of the Golden Horde. Such empires developed their own characteristics, which often incorporated outside influences left behind by conquerors or imported by traders – such as the trans-Saharan caravaners, or Persian sailors navigating the southern sea lanes of the Silk Route. Other civilisations continued to exist in fragmented isolation, such as the Aborigines of Australia and the native tribes of North America.

Like the economist Friedman's San Francisco, all stages of human development existed on the same horizontal timeline. Each of these contained their own kernel of uniqueness, yet none more so than the next empire we will consider. This would evolve its own version of sophistication, untouched by developments elsewhere. Indeed, its very existence leads us to question the inevitability, or otherwise, of human evolution.

Were we bound to become what we are? Is it in our genes, something foretold in our social interaction, something intrinsic to the very nature of society itself? What does far-flung humanity retain in common? Such questions are necessarily raised by the very existence of the Aztec Empire. The culture, mores and entire social structure of this empire, which evolved in the isolation of Mesoamerica, prompts all manner of undermining inquiry.

The Aztec Empire

Like the Mongol Empire, the Aztec Empire was brief and bloodthirsty, after which its influences were all but expunged from the surface of history. However, deeper cultural resonances would remain unacknowledged. Perhaps the most striking image of this comes from its sister civilisation, the Inca Empire, which developed independently on the western littoral of South America.

Some years after the conquest of the Incas by Spain, a young Catholic priest newly arrived from his home country was conducting a service in a local cathedral. Looking down at the dimly lit rows of Inca faces of his supposedly converted congregation, he recognised that despite appearances, they were in fact still practising their ancient religion. Indeed, they had even decorated the cathedral in such a fashion that Christ, the Virgin Mary and the statues of the saints had all taken on the guise of Inca gods. The sudden realisation by this callow priest that he was unwittingly officiating at the rites of a dark deity, of whose pagan mysteries he knew nothing, had such a traumatic effect on him that he suffered a mental breakdown.

Like its short-lived Mongol contemporary on the other

side of the globe, the Aztec Empire was also riven with contradictions quite as gruesome as any Mongol atrocity. An epitome of Aztec art can be seen in the eerily beautiful yet chilling life-sized skulls, which were carved out of single pieces of transparent quartz. The diaphanous interior markings of the crystal inside the glass-like skulls were believed to contain the secrets of the early history and final destiny of humanity.

Several of these skulls belonging to prestigious national collections, such as the superb skull in the British Museum, have been demonstrated to be skilful centuries-old fakes. Yet such is their power, which surely mimics the originals from which they were copied, that the authorities have for the most part taken the exceptional step of leaving them on display.

Less chillingly skilled, yet equally original, is the cartoon-like art produced by the Aztecs, drawn on stretched deer-skin or dried sisal leaves (agave fibre). These recorded scenes from Aztec history have a similar compelling veracity, though entirely different style, to those of the Bayeux Tapestry, which recorded the Norman invasion of England in 1066. Though unlike the Bayeux Tapestry, these have been assembled together as codices, or books, such as the Codex Mendoza.

As this name suggests, the original Aztec artefacts were only made into books following the Spanish conquest. Originally these drawings appeared on long, carefully folded-up sheets of material, and would have told their stories in similar fashion to the lengths of material that make up the Bayeux Tapestry. Included in the Aztec codices are such wonders as a man watching a comet pass through the heavens, and numerous examples of the exotic costumes and headdresses worn on ceremonial occasions, frequently adorned with brightly coloured feathers from local macaws and birds of paradise.

By contrast, many of the drawings depict scenes of unspeakable horror, at least to Western eyes. Cartoons depict men gathered together enjoying parties of ritual cannibalism; a still-living human, gazing up as his recently cut out heart is held aloft gushing blood; examples of 'auto-sacrifice', involving 'synchronised blood-letting', where the participants pierced their bodies with cactus spines.

Aztec ritual human sacrifice, cutting out
the heart of the living victim.

Even in daily life, simple beauty often coexisted along-side excruciating barbarity. This was a society whose currency was chocolate, yet to pay the gods for keeping them alive, their ritual mass slaughters unleashed waves of blood that spilled down the steps of their towering pyramids.

What is it about quasi-pyramidal structures and their apparent ubiquity in early societies? The Aztec pyramids were not like the classic Egyptian pyramids, yet they bore an uncanny resemblance to Babylonian ziggurats. The Chinese also built pyramidal structures – the mound that housed the Emperor Qin's terracotta army bears a certain resemblance to one, which may have been more striking when it was first erected. As do the ancient Buddhist stupas of India, the earliest of which date from the fourth century BC. And just a few decades ago, some Chinese archaeologists came across a 5,000-year-old stepped pyramid in the remote mountains of Mongolia.

Babylon, Egypt, Mexico, China, India, now Mongolia – and perhaps even more examples waiting to be discovered in other remote parts of the globe . . . is the building of pyramids somehow a universal stage of human development? In many of the above cases, there can have been no possible contact between the people who built these pyramids. Does this mean that there is something in our common history that prompts civilisations at a certain stage in their development to expend the enormous effort required to erect such massive objects? Is this shape some kind of archetype, which lurks at a subconscious level of the human mind?

The twentieth-century Swiss psychologist, Carl Jung, who based his understanding of the human mind upon the existence of a collective unconscious containing such archetypes, would certainly have us believe so. Yet there exists no rigid scientific method to test such a theory. So what is the significance of this shape in humanity's disparate history – a shape whose appearance is often separated by thousands of miles and thousands of years?

The earliest Mesopotamian stepped ziggurats date from around 3000 BC. The earliest Egyptian pyramids, which were similarly stepped, date from around 2750 BC, and may well have been copied from their Mesopotamian counterparts. The recently discovered and similarly stepped pyramid found in Mongolia seems to have been contemporary with these distant artefacts. Yet despite any resemblance, it certainly could not have been copied from its counterparts in the Fertile Crescent. The earliest Mesoamerican pyramids are thought to date from anything up to 1000 BC. But there could have been no external influence here either. So is all this part of a human trait, or mere coincidence?

Try looking at this question from another point of view. What are the shapes of other great isolated ancient or prehistoric structures? Do they bear any resemblance to pyramids, or even to each other? Just a brief list of these would seem to dispel such psychological speculation. The large Stone Faces (Moai) of Easter Island, the Walls of Zimbabwe, Stonehenge, Angkor Wat, Timbuktu – each of these isolated monuments is unique in construction and form, and had its subtle differences of purpose, too. The pyramid, it seems, is not an archetype – more part of a primitive inclination, only one of many instincts that prompted early human society to build monuments greater than the individual human being.

Although we do not always know the precise purpose of these structures, we can surmise that they somehow represented their society, or its leader, or were vital in the performance of some sacred function for the people who erected them – possibly reminding them of a near-forgotten mythical past, or the mountainous landscape of their original homeland.

Which brings us to the question of who the Aztecs were, and where they came from. The Aztecs spoke a group of closely related languages known as Nahuatal. During the time of the Aztec Empire, this was a largely verbal language. The only permanent records were what we now call the codices, which consisted largely of drawings. However, there is evidence that they also contained writing in pictographs and ideograms, as well as a surprisingly sophisticated number system.

Unfortunately, the codices that have come down to us are for the most part corrupted European versions, which included various commentaries. The unadulterated originals were seemingly all destroyed by the Christian invaders, who regarded them as nothing more than pagan texts. Even so, the remaining neo-codices do contain a number of scenes depicting divination, Aztec ceremonies, and ritual calendars, as well as representations of the gods. However, the most reliable and uncorrupted of the several versions of the Aztec origin myth existed only in the purely verbal Nahuatal form.

According to this, at the time of the creation there was a god called Ometecuhtli, which translates as 'twice a deity'. He existed in male and female form and produced four sons. Two of these – Quetzalcoatl and Huitzilopochtli – were given the task of bringing into existence other lesser gods with specific duties, as well as creating the earth and all its people. With the birth of these early four gods, there began a series of historical cycles of creation and destruction related to the sun. During the Aztec Empire and its preceding history there had been four suns, each of which had been destroyed by a catastrophic event. Nahuatal text records: 'We now live in the time of the fifth sun.'

The people of this era worshipped Quetzalcoatl, the god of light and air, who had rescued humanity after the fourth sun had been destroyed by Tezcatlipoca, god of judgement, darkness and sorcery. In order to appease Tezcatlipoca, and prevent him inflicting another catastrophe, he had to be paid off, nourished with the blood of human sacrifice. If this was not sufficient, he would turn the sun black, the world would be rent asunder in a violent earthquake, and Tzitzimitl, the goddess of the stars, would slay all of humanity.

Just as intriguing is the actual origin of the Aztec people. This leads us back to the very first of our species and their initial migrations out of Africa, a narrative that unearths some surprising facts, as well as a number of unanswered questions about this period of human prehistory. The first hominids are known to have begun emigrating from Africa around two million years ago. The earliest of these was Homo erectus, who was followed over many millennia by other archaic hominids such as Denisovans and Neanderthals, both sub-species of the genus Homo. All of these species are now extinct; although, as we shall see, elements of them live on in an unexpected fashion.

Our own particular species, Homo sapiens, evolved in East Africa over 200,000 years ago as a separate member of the hominid family. Its one apparent advantage was the size of its cranial capacity. Where Neanderthals and others had a capacity of just under 1,000 cc, Homo sapiens initially had a capacity of around 1,300 cc, though most of this was unused. Almost certainly on account of failing crops (climate change) and consequent territorial competition, groups of Homo sapiens left their native East Africa some 75,000 years ago, following in the footsteps of their hominid predecessors.

These groups of Homo sapiens, which seem to have consisted of as few as 1,000 individuals, are known to have left Africa by two routes – via the Sinai peninsula, as well as across the southern Red Sea Strait to Yemen. As these small groups began to multiply and spread out through Asia and later Europe, they are known to have interbred with the hominid subspecies that preceded them. Consequently, the modern humans who inhabit Asia and Europe still contain around 1 to 2 per cent Neanderthal DNA.

It seems that little interbreeding took place in Africa itself, as the modern African populations who did not migrate contain practically no Neanderthal DNA, and are thus much purer Homo sapiens, a fact that gives the lie to much spurious racialist theory. In fact, one consequence of Homo sapiens interbreeding with his cousin hominids who had preceded him into more northerly latitudes, which had regular cold seasons, was that it enabled him to adapt to those barren periods of the year when nothing grew.

It took Homo sapiens around 20,000 years to spread east as far as China and Siberia. Here the picture becomes blurred. In the twentieth century, evidence of a 750,000-year-old Homo erectus, named Peking Man, was discovered in China. The twentieth-century German anthropologist, Franz Weidenreich, 'considered Peking Man as a human ancestor and especially an ancestor of the Chinese people'. To this day, the Chinese are taught in school textbooks that they are evolved directly from Peking Man, and not from the group of Homo sapiens who evolved in East Africa.

This claim remains controversial and widely disputed amongst many non-Chinese anthropologists. Whether or not this has any more veracity than the Chinese claim to have discovered Australia remains beside the point. Here again we have the notion of 'ethos' entering history. Concepts such as those implicit in the Peking Man theory have similarities reaching back through all of world history. This is a classic claim of racial 'difference' (frequently implying superiority) such as has preceded, time and again, a justification for empire. As we shall see, this remains as true in the so-called 'post-imperial' period as it was during the long era of empires that preceded it.

To which we now return. As we have seen, the rulers of empire are not only the victors, but see themselves as a superior people – either racially, and/or culturally. An early example of the latter was Alexander the Great's attempt to 'conquer the world'. His declared aim was to impose on his conquered lands the advanced and superior culture of Ancient Greece (of which he had only a tentative grasp, having paid little attention during his youth to the lessons he was given by his private tutor, Aristotle).

A similar belief inspired the Soviet Union's imposition of communism on the nations of Eastern Europe: capitalism was a spent force, the future lay in the Leninist-Marxist approach. The elephant in the room here, of course, is Hitler's drive to impose on the world 'a thousand year

Reich', an enterprise which falls into both categories of supposed superiority, i.e. racial and cultural.

Some 25,000 years ago, when the first bands of paleolithic hunter-gatherers reached the far north-eastern corner of Siberia, they were inspired by no such inflated ideas of empire. Survival was their main concern. By now the earth was in the grip of the Last Ice Age. With so much water locked in solid ice, the sea levels were some 400 feet lower than they are today, leaving the Beringa Land Bridge joining north-eastern Siberia to north-west Alaska above sea level.[27]

It is thought that at least three separate waves of hunter-gatherers crossed the Beringa Land Bridge, causing these original inhabitants of the Americas to spread with surprising rapidity through the north and then to the south of the American landmass. What is believed to be the origins of a 21,000-year-old camp fire have been discovered in Mexico. By 8000 BC, the indigenous inhabitants of Mexico had begun to cultivate maize (corn), whose plentiful crops and easy storage would play an integral role in Mesoamerican development, both cultural and agricultural.

This nourishing and easily cultivated grain aided the growth of a series of civilisations, which grew up in Mesoamerica from sometime around 2600 BC. Amongst the most important of these were the early Olmecs (*c.* 1400–400 BC). These inhabited the tropical terrain and hinterland

---

27 Indeed, many present-day global features were radically different. Japan was joined to Korea and China, and a land bridge between Europe and Asia separated the Black Sea from the Mediterranean. These and other geographical transformations give pause for thought concerning early racial development, as well as the future sea-level rise that will be caused by global warming. The world was not, and will not, always be the same. Either geographically, or politically.

of southern Mexico on the border of the Caribbean. Today these people are best remembered for their huge, stone carved heads, which appear to be a realistic representation of a people with square heads, broad noses and wide lips, with fleshy but intimidating features.

This close resemblance to native African features led some early historians to speculate that the Olmecs must have arrived directly across the Atlantic from Africa, but DNA testing has disproved this theory. The Olmecs developed a hieroglyphic script, believed to be the earliest in Mesoamerica, as well as an advanced mathematics used to calculate calendars and the movement of the stars. On the other hand, they also introduced the ritual practice of blood-letting described earlier – self-stabbing to produce blood and appease the gods.

Around the half century prior to 350 BC, the Olmecs went into a sudden decline. Entire cities were abandoned, and the population diminished rapidly. Historians have tended to put this down to a series of violent eruptions that took place in the region around this period. However, many elements of Olmec civilisation would pass on to successive Mesoamerican civilisations. With hindsight, we can see that the Olmecs played a formative role in the evolution of the Aztecs.

The other dominant civilisation in the region were the Maya, who co-existed with the Olmecs, flourishing between 1800 BC and AD 250. The Mayan territory lay to the south-east of the Olmecs, straddling the wide swathe of the Mesoamerican peninsula from Yucatan to the north and the Pacific Ocean to the south. Inevitably there was conflict between these two neighbouring territories. Apart from the exotic feathered decorations of the combatants, these battles were primitive affairs, fought in Stone-Age style with spears, stone axes and hurled stones. Warriors were bedecked in coloured feathers and their leaders would wear feathered headgear. Not until around 380 BC were more modern weapons introduced. (In fact, these were secrets stolen from the Tenochtitlan, inhabitants of a powerful city state that occupied central Mexico.)

This advanced technology consisted of slings, spears tipped with sharp obsidian blades, as well as wooden shields, helmets made of strong hide, and upper armour tailored from animal skins. Even with the introduction of such new weapons, the battles remained somewhat primitive. The secrets of making iron, and constructing a wheel, let alone a chariot, remained unknown. This meant that battles were fought with little strategy in mind. Armies would form in line opposite one another, and then charge. Thus, according to the twentieth-century South African anthropologist, David Webster, such battles soon descended into anarchy, with much 'thrusting, stabbing, and crushing'.

Almost all men in Mayan society were trained as warriors, and were esteemed according to the ferocity with which they fought. This was the only means by which Mayans could rise in social status. However, the object in battle was not to kill your opponent, but to capture him alive. Prisoners thus taken would be used as human sacrifices in the ceremonies conducted to appease the gods.

The only exception to this warrior class were the priests. It was believed that they could communicate directly with the gods, or act as an intermediary between a citizen and his chosen god. More significantly, the Mayans developed their own language, which was more sophisticated than Olmec. Unlike previous Mesoamerican languages, which consisted of pictographs (standardised drawings resembling objects), the Mayans developed a script consisting of ideograms (symbols standing for ideas). This crossed the threshold from being a pictorial recording system to a sophisticated language, capable of conveying a much more subtle expression of thought.

Like the Olmecs, the Mayans also built impressive pyramids. However, the Mayan pyramids tend to be shorter, with a larger area at the summit. Experts have concluded that this was to enable the construction of a temple, or perhaps to accommodate larger human sacrifices. The Mayans also developed their own distinctive method of stone carving, for both statues and friezes. Investigations of the movements of the stars and the change of the seasons led the priests to develop their own mathematical system. As distinct from our present decimal system (based on ten numbers), the Mayan system was vigesimal, i.e. based on twenty numbers (counting both fingers and toes).

The Mayans also invented, and inserted into their calculations, a symbol for zero. This was an astonishing feat. Zero was, and remains, a particularly slippery concept to grasp. It was *something* that represented *nothing*.[28] The Mayan symbol for zero was an empty tortoise shell. According to the contemporary US historian, John Justeson: 'This may have been the earliest known occurrence of the idea of an explicit zero worldwide.' A number of experts contest this, some claiming the Babylonians as the first,

---

28 It can also more practically be used as a placeholder, indicating that there are no numbers in a particular column. For example, in our decimal system the placeholder o in the number 702 shows that there are no numbers in the 'tens' column.

others the Indians. Interestingly, this symbol did not reach China until the fourth century AD, while it was not until the early 1100s that it passed to Europe from Arabic culture.

Here is a prime example of sideways history; yet it also serves as a prime example of a concept remaining undeveloped. The Mayans found no need to make further use of their newly discovered zero. The Europeans, who were entering the age of widespread foreign exchange and banking, certainly did, and benefitted accordingly. This led to a great leap forward in European mathematical understanding, as well as facilitating mercantile interaction.

The collapse of Mayan civilisation was as mysterious as it was sudden. After a continuous history of over 2,000 years, Mayan life rapidly began to disintegrate. Between the end of the eighth century AD and the beginning of the ninth century AD, the Mayans began to desert their cities, as well as the pasturelands they had painstakingly carved out of the tropical rainforest. The jungle reclaimed most of these sites, but cities and ancient pyramids are still being discovered to this day. Aerial mapping techniques used in Guatemala and the Yucatan peninsula (Mexico) indicate the existence of large networks of freshwater canals, farming on an industrial scale, and extensive cities with pyramids, temples and plazas.

It was out of this rich mix of Mesoamerican civilisations that the Aztecs would finally emerge as the major empire. In 1428, a triple alliance was formed between the three most powerful city states in central Mexico: Tenochtitlan, Texcoco, and Tlacopan. This new Aztec power base soon reduced their neighbours to 'tribute' states, until the empire extended across central Mexico from the Caribbean to the Pacific, around 500 miles at its widest.

The capital of this new empire was the fabled city of Tenochtitlan, on the present site of Mexico City. When Tenochtitlan was founded, this region was covered by the shallow waters of Lake Texcoco. The land chosen for the city was a marshy offshore island – hardly a promising location, despite its protection by the surrounding waters. The island was drained, easily defensible causeways were linked to the mainland, and terracotta ducts brought fresh water from surrounding springs and rivers. The city itself was built on a semi-grid pattern, with well laid-out canals, causeways, streets, plazas, temples and pyramids. Within just over a century, this city had become one of the wonders of the world. Its population was said to have been over 300,000, making it far larger than any city in Europe, matched only by the likes of Hangzhou and Cairo.

To anyone mounting the hillside overlooking the lake for the first time, Tenochtitlan appeared like a dream, or at least a mirage island in the midst of the still waters of the lake. Inside the city, the streets were filled with a people whose migrating ancestors had parted over seventy millennia ago from the Homo sapiens who had evolved to become the European variety of the species.

In the marketplaces, the short, stocky stallholders had square, light-brown faces, fringed, straight black hair, and wore rudimentary clothes made out of dried maguey (agave) leaf-fibres. Their stalls were heaped with colourful foodstuffs seen nowhere else on earth: maize, peppers, sweet potatoes, peanuts, cocoa beans, vanilla pods. The citizens lived with their families in small huts made of wattle and daub, along with their domesticated dogs and pet turkeys. To entertain themselves, they sat on the ground playing flutes, whose whistles were echoed by the exotic-coloured parrots who perched on the rooftops.

Most amazing of all was the palace of the king, which contained over a thousand rooms, each with its own bath. His gardens contained no less than two separate zoos – one containing eagles and birds of prey, whilst the second housed large wild cats with leopard-like markings on their fur (ocelots) and ferocious-looking black dragon-like reptiles with crests on their backs (iguanas). Elsewhere in the garden, ducks with all manner of colourful plumage swam in more than a dozen ponds.

Yet at the heart of this wondrous city lay its ceremonial centre, complete with sacrificial pyramids, where the citizens would gather to watch the gruesome blood-letting for the gods. Curiously, the victims who took part in these horrific ceremonies appear to have been led up the steps quite calmly, and to have accepted their living disembowelment with an equanimity that is all but impossible for us to conceive. It has been suggested that they must have been drugged beforehand, but contemporary evidence contradicts this.

Following the sacrifice, the victims 'were sent rolling down the steps of the temple, and the steps were bathed in blood'. The gore and bodies tumbling down the steps of the pyramids towards the population below seem to have evoked similar alien emotions. One would expect the assembled crowd to experience a mix of strong contradictory feelings. Fear and empathy, reinforcing the dominance of the authorities – such as was experienced at public executions in empires elsewhere. Or a warped exultation at the death of so many enemies. Perhaps catharsis even, as was experienced by the audience at an Ancient Greek tragedy.

No, the Aztecs appear to have accepted that such bloodshed was necessary to feed the gods, as well as to maintain the all-important business of assisting the sun on its course, in order to prevent any catastrophe such as might bring their present era to an end.

After the ceremonies, the skulls of those who had been sacrificed were stacked in racks outside the temples. As to the precise numbers of those sacrificed, figures remain uncertain. When a new temple to Huitzilopochtli, the fearsome god of the sun and war, was dedicated in 1487, it is said that 80,400 people (including women and children) were sacrificed. This is certainly an exaggeration. On the other hand, scholars agree that as many as 20,000 victims may have been sacrificed each year throughout the empire, both around this time and during the preceding decades.

Yet now that the three main city states had formed an alliance, there was less occasion for war, and consequently a lack of captives for the human sacrifice ceremony. And even a succession of minor wars against nearby vassal states could only provide an increasingly inadequate supply. In 1450 there was a severe famine, and according to the twentieth-century Mexican anthropologist, Miguel Leon-Portilla, the priests declared that 'the gods were angry at the empire and to placate them it was necessary to sacrifice many men and this had to be done regularly.'

To overcome this problem, the authorities arranged so-called 'Battles of the Flowers'. Far from being as innocuous and enchanting as their name might suggest, these consisted of ritual battles between chosen members of the different city states. Lethal weapons were substituted with flat wooden clubs, which could batter the enemy into submission, perhaps even render him unconscious, so that he could be captured without sustaining serious injury. These battles had the added advantage of providing military training, as well as supplying sacrificial victims.

All this would seem to indicate a population with an all-pervasive aura of collectivity, to the point where it seemingly obliterated any ill-defined remnant of individuality amongst its citizens. Yet this was far from being the case: the Aztecs had developed their own unique sense of self. According to George Orwell, writing of his contemporaries: 'By the age of fifty every man has the face he deserves.' Well over half a millennium previously, the Aztecs had refined this casual generalisation into a profound individualistic philosophy of their own. This way of thought had originally been developed by the privileged class of 'wise men' amongst the priesthood, who claimed that it stemmed from 'the legendary symbol of Nahuatl knowledge – the great figure of Quetzalcoatl'. The latter god appeared in the form of a feathered serpent and was responsible for the creation of humanity. According to his teachings, it should be the aim of all men 'to have and develop in themselves *a face*'. This eliminated the anonymity into which they had been born, and enabled them to 'put a mirror before their fellow men'. It enabled each human being to develop self-knowledge, wisdom and care – both for himself, his family and his people.

So profound was this message that it was said its implications were embodied in the Nahuatl language itself. Western philosophers will recognise a poetic version of the teachings of Socrates in the initial urge to self-knowledge. As for the second part, the idea that the very language we learn leads us to the philosophical conclusions we reach, is astonishingly modern. Not until the twentieth century would the Austrian linguistic philosopher Wittgenstein suggest this paradox.

In 1502, the thirty-six-year-old Montezuma II succeeded as the ninth ruler of Tenochtitlan, holding sway over the entire Aztec Empire. Montezuma II was renowned as a warrior and is said to have extended the influence of his empire to its greatest limits. Others speak of him as being indecisive and overwhelmed by a foreboding of his own tragic destiny. The early years of his reign witnessed a number of omens prophesying disaster. Then a comet was observed, marking for many the end of the fifty-two-year cycle of the Aztec calendar, and the imminence of the end of the fifth sun.

When Christopher Columbus made landfall in the Americas in 1492, this isolated landmass was once again reunited with the outside world. The Spanish immediately launched a full-scale search and conquest in the hope of extracting precious metals and other valuables. Backed by such motives, the Spanish conquistador, Hernán Cortés, made landfall in February 1519 on the Mexican coast at what is now Puerto Cruz. He was accompanied by just five hundred men. According to an ancient belief stemming from the Tolmec era, the gods had sailed from Mexico, promising that they would one day return.

Cortés and his men seemed to fulfil this prophecy. To the Aztecs they even resembled gods: the Europeans had white skin and fearsome beards, some were giants with two arms and four legs (men on horseback), and they could kill people far away from them with a bang and a puff of smoke (musket-fire). Amazingly, the Aztecs had built their huge and precisely constructed monuments without the use of pack animals or the wheel.

Just as the Europeans had never seen tomatoes, potatoes and the like, the Aztecs in their isolation had developed no immunity to such common European diseases as smallpox, cholera, bubonic plague, 'flu and even the common cold. On the other hand, Spanish sailors returning to Europe brought with them the scourge of syphilis. The collapse of the already ailing Aztec Empire was as swift as it was spectacular.

Within two years, Cortés and his few hundred men had, by means of trickery, propaganda, superior weaponry, disease and so forth overcome the Aztec Empire. In the process Montezuma II was held hostage and killed, Tenochtitlan was destroyed, and Cortés inadvertently became the first European to set eyes on the western Pacific Ocean. Up to three million Aztecs are said to have died, and the rest were converted to Christianity by Catholic priests, with results we have already described. To this day, in remote jungle regions of the Yucatan Peninsula, Honduras, and Guatemala, isolated tribes of Mayan and Aztec people are known to continue with their own indigenous cultural practices.

Sequence

Concurrent with the Aztec Empire was the Inca Empire, which at its height occupied the remote east coast and hinterland of South America from the southmost tip of Colombia as far as mid-Chile, a distance of some 2,500 miles. In isolation, this too had developed into an original civilisation, quite independently of the Aztecs. The Inca's wealth, and their downfall, resulted largely from Potosi, the so-called 'mountain of silver', which soon attracted the attention of the Spanish conquistador, Francisco Pizzaro, who led just 160 men and conquered the empire in two years. However, he never discovered the empire's masterpiece, the so-called 'lost city of the Incas'. This was Machu Picchu, built over 8,000 feet up in the Peruvian Andes, by a civilisation that had only llamas (worthless as pack animals over mountainous terrain), and like the Aztecs had yet to discover the wheel. Machu Picchu would remain 'lost' for another 400 years.

However, in 1553 the Spanish did discover an ancient artefact, which remains as impressive and perplexing as any yet found on earth. Some 1,700 feet up in the Peruvian Andes they came across a long, permanently dry, windless, arid plateau covered in drawings known as the Nazca Lines. These depict in outline vast geoglyphs – drawings of plants, animals, even spiders, and primitive representations of human-like creatures with round heads, eyes and legs. And a number of seemingly unknown creatures. As well as these there are a series of undeviating straight lines, some over 1,000 feet long, which have been drawn across the desert floor.

It appears that these all date from around 200 and 600 BC. Yet despite all manner of ingenious explanations, no serious investigator has yet managed to provide any entirely convincing explanation of their existence. By contrast, the irrepressible Erich von Däniken has asserted that these markings were created by 'ancient astronauts'. Despite such tomfoolery, there is no denying that the full beauty and art of these markings can only fully be appreciated when they are viewed from high in the sky, and are even visible from satellites.

Such pre-modern imperial wonders appear all the more amazing when seen in the larger historical context of the migration of Homo sapiens to the very limits of the habitable globe. The challenges encountered on these migrations had led to Homo sapiens mastering a series of entirely new cognitive skills. As we have seen, the manifestations of these developments bore both perplexing similarities and astonishing differences. Yet in a profound sense, they were common throughout the species. They involved traits capable of abstract, symbolic and religious behaviour. This was the beginnings of art, science and writing. Humanity as we know it had been born.

But this new variant species was far from being any Nietzschean 'superman' in comparison with his fellow hominids. Homo sapiens may have been taller than Homo erectus and others, but many of these – especially Neanderthals – were much stockier and physically stronger. Threats from early hominids, climate change, geography and all the 'accidents of history' ensured that the family groups and tribes of these new, more advanced beings were constantly on the move, driven further and further from their home continent. Yet their developing superior faculties, ingenuity in adapting to their surroundings, and imagination, ensured that they thrived and continued to evolve.

On attaining the furthest habitable limits of our planet, they often found hominid predecessors in residence. These two 'cousin' species would live alongside each other, on occasion for many thousands of years. Yet in every known case, Homo sapiens seems to have outlived its hominid predecessors, who became extinct. The speed with which this new Homo sapiens spread across our planet is remarkable. A brief (and much simplified) list will suffice to illustrate this.

Although the first human immigrants crossed the Beringa Land Bridge from Eastern Siberia some 25,000 years ago, within 9,000 years they had reached Patagonia at the tip of South America. Just 2,000 years after this, a second wave of migrants crossed the bridge, peopling the North American plains with groups of indigenous tribespeople. It was another 10,000 years before a third wave, the Inuits, arrived and took possession of the icy wastes of northern Canada.

Homo sapiens arrived comparatively early in western Australia, some 65,000 years ago. Yet it was just 3,000 years ago that a late wave of seafaring people set off into the Pacific, travelling north of Australia via New Guinea. After this they split, populating the Pacific islands. The northern group reached Hawaii around 1,000 years ago, the southern group reached New Zealand around the same time. These latter people then continued east along a distended line of islands until finally they reached the very last of the chain, now known as Easter Island, around AD 300, but possibly as late as AD 1200.[29]

Here they started erecting almost a thousand tall stone heads (Moai), all facing east. These remain only one of the many unsolved mysteries concerning this island, which is around 1,000 miles from the nearest islands (the Pitcairns) and over 2,000 miles from the coast of South America, making it one of the most remote inhabited spots on earth. It would be at least half a millennium before the island was rediscovered by Europeans, who arrived to find

---

29 Even the latest scientific evidence is conflicting on this point.

the natives harvesting sweet potatoes, which originate from South America, suggesting that the inhabitants had American origins. On the other hand, the Europeans' ship also had a Hawaiian crew member, who was able to communicate with the locals by means of his own language.

This now brings us up to date with the population of the earth by Homo sapiens. However, this in itself leads to an intriguing question concerning our species. Namely, its ability to produce art: an impulse that would increasingly characterise individual human development from this period on in far-flung regions ranging from Renaissance Europe to Moghul India and Ming China.

Once again, it is necessary to return to prehistoric times. As we have seen, the impulse to create pyramids was not universal. Yet Homo sapiens does appear to have been driven by a compulsive need to leave behind him a precise trace of his existence, which can be seen as the beginnings of art. And what is most striking is the very particularity that this impulse first took: hand stencils. These were created by placing a hand on a cave wall and blowing coloured pigment (such as red ochre) through a pipe so that the outlined imprint of the hand remained. This is arguably the earliest form of individualised art, yet its widespread and spontaneously independent appearance in vastly disparate locations is revelatory.

Such stencils appeared in caves in France and Spain (dating from some 35,000 years ago). Identical stencils appear as far apart as Indonesia (40,000 years ago) and Patagonia (9,000 years ago). But there is a sting in the tail. Such artefacts appeared to demonstrate a quality unique to Homo sapiens, until in 2018 hand stencils were found in caves in Spain, which predated the emigration of Homo sapiens from Africa by some 20,000 years. And these hands were unmistakably Neanderthal.

Homo sapiens is certainly unique amongst the hominids[30] in having survived extinction. Which begs the question: what else is unique about the evolution of this species apart from its survival, along with the lasting monuments of empire that it left behind?

---

30 In the limited understanding of this species, i.e. excluding great apes, gorillas, etc.

The Ottoman Empire

We now return to the region where the world's earliest empires had begun – and thrived – for almost three millennia, namely the Middle East. The Ottoman Empire, which originated in 1299, would eventually achieve sovereignty over territory in Asia, Europe and Africa, and would last for over 600 years. On four remarkable occasions it would even threaten to destroy the more advanced civilisation of Europe. Just 150 years after the founding declaration of the Ottoman Empire, during its early expansionist phase, Sultan Mehmed II (usually known as 'the Conqueror') achieved the unthinkable feat of conquering Constantinople, the capital of the Byzantine Empire (still officially designated the 'Roman and Byzantine Empire').

At its height in the eleventh century, the Byzantine Empire had ruled over every country bordering on the Mediterranean, from Spain and Italy to Egypt and North Africa, as well as controlling the shores of the Black Sea and the upper half of the Red Sea. By 1453, Mehmed the Conqueror had all but destroyed this empire, taking Anatolia, Greece and moving up into the Balkans, in the process encircling Constantinople. After Mehmed the

Conqueror entered the holy city, Constantine XI, the last man to claim the title of Roman Emperor, was killed.

The Ottoman sultan then declared that the 900-year-old Hagia Sofia ('Holy Wisdom' in Greek), Christendom's holiest cathedral and the largest building in the world, would from now on become a mosque. He also pronounced himself 'Kaysari-i-Rûm' (Turkish for 'Caesar of Rome'). From his vantage point on the Bosphorus, Mehmed the Conqueror's capital straddled Europe and Asia, making it the potential capital of the world. (Just over three centuries later, when Napoleon took Egypt, harbouring similar illusions, he regarded Cairo as the most strategic city on earth, the hub of Europe, Asia and Africa; America was dismissed as a primitive outpost.)

Back in Rome, a succession of popes had desperately been attempting to rally the divided nations of European Christendom to restart the Crusades, and drive back the Ottomans. One by one these attempts foundered, owing to ineffectual leadership, internal jealousies, suspicions and so forth. Meanwhile the Ottoman advance continued inexorably north through the Balkans towards Venice, and in 1480 even established a foothold on the Italian peninsula at the southern port of Otranto. Here the local bishop was publicly sawn in half before the terrified population, 12,000 of whom were then put to the sword, with another 50,000 being shipped off into slavery.

Within weeks, the Ottoman forces had advanced 200 miles up the east coast. Less than 200 miles east across the Apennines, the ailing, ageing Pope Sixtus IV was at his wits' end. It looked as if Rome was now to suffer the fate of Constantinople. Then, as if by a miracle, the Ottomans suddenly withdrew and sailed back across the Adriatic. In an echo of the Mongol invasion of Eastern Europe three centuries previously, the Ottomans had learned of the death of Mehmed the Conqueror, and were anxious to return to Constantinople where the future sultan would be chosen. Europe was saved.

But the threat of the Ottomans overrunning Europe was not over. Within fifty years, Sultan Suleiman the Magnificent was laying siege to the city of Vienna. But the autumn of 1529 was long and wet, and the Turkish troops soon became demoralised, their supply lines were overstretched, and a collapse of morale led to a Turkish retreat. Yet 150 years later, Sultan Mehmed IV ordered a second attempt to take Vienna, this time with a fully equipped and supplied army of 200,000 men, led by the Grand Vizier (chief minister) Kara Mustafa Pasha.

In July 1683, before the Turks were even within sight of Vienna, the ruling Holy Roman Emperor, Leopold I, and 60,000 of its citizens had fled. In fact, Leopold I's act was less cowardly than it appeared – his intention was to solicit support from Poland, Cossacks and German allies. The massive Ottoman Army duly laid siege to Vienna, digging trenches and setting up tents in preparation for a long winter. By now the Ottoman Empire had considerably expanded its territory, stretching along the North African coast, through Egypt, Arabia, Syria, Iraq as far as the Caspian Sea. In Europe it had overrun the Balkans, Romania and Hungary. Once Vienna fell, the whole of central and western Europe would lie at its mercy.

The Ottoman forces had soon overrun the outer fortifications of Vienna, and were beginning to dig tunnels beneath its walls. Then, on 12 September, the Ottomans were surprised by the appearance of a combined German-

Polish force, which emerged from the Vienna Woods at Mount Kahlenberg to the north of the city. The ensuing battle lasted fifteen hours, before the tent of the Grand Vizier was detonated, and as his troops fled from their trenches they were put to the slaughter. Kara Mustafa managed to make it to the safety of Belgrade, but the sultan was so outraged that he ordered his Grand Vizier to be executed, and his head brought to Constantinople on a silver dish. The battle of Kahlenberg is generally seen as marking the turning point of the Ottoman Empire, and from now on it would begin its long decline.

Ironically, it was this long decline that would have the most profound effect of all: presaging both the ultimate disintegration of the Ottoman Empire and the political destruction of the old European order. By the nineteenth century, the Ottoman Empire was an impotent force. Egypt was virtually independent under the Mamlukes, Persia and the Kurds threatened its eastern borders, Greece would declare itself independent in 1853; and Czar Nicholas I of Russia described Turkey as 'the sick old man of Europe'. Here was a vast empire ready for the taking, and all the European powers were covertly making plans to seize strategic territories for themselves.

As early as 1799, Napoleon had already taken Egypt, but within a couple of years the British navy forced the French to return home. The British then came to an arrangement with the Porte (Ottoman government in Istanbul), whereby they would act as Egypt's 'protector'. However, this did not deter Napoleon. Having declared himself 'Emperor', he began covertly drawing up plans for an overland invasion of Turkey, in an attempt to forestall the Russians, who had by now extended their empire into the Caucasus borderland and looked poised to launch their own invasion.

Things came to a head with the outbreak of the Crimean War in 1853, between Russia and an alliance of the Ottomans, Britain, France and Sardinia. The ostensible cause of this war was a dispute between Roman Catholic and Russian Orthodox monks over the keys to the door of the Church of the Nativity in Bethlehem (Christ's birthplace). The underlying cause was to prevent Russia from expanding into the Ottoman Empire, an aim in which the western European allies eventually succeeded after a chaotic campaign involving great loss of life.

Determined not to be left out, in the early 1900s the recently formed German nation persuaded the sultan to allow their engineers to construct a Hejaz railway from Damascus to Medina, ostensibly for the transport of pilgrims making the Hadj to Mecca. But in fact, as all could see, this railway would become an integral part of an interlinked Berlin to Baghdad railway, a key piece of German strategy.

The Hejaz railway could be extended to Aqaba on the Red Sea, while the Baghdad branch could be extended to the head of the Persian Gulf. This would enable the Germans direct access to the Indian Ocean, thus circumventing the British-French owned Suez Canal, and enabling the Germans to extend their own empire beyond the bounds of German East Africa (basically mainland modern Tanzania). By the turn of the twentieth century, the strategic European rivalries were falling into place, indicating many of the locations that in 1914 would become the flashpoints of the First World War.

Such thumbnail sketches of the rise and fall of one of

history's greatest empires give little indication of the transformation of the world that took place around it. During the years between 1299 and the Ottoman collapse in 1922 the world changed as never before, shifting beyond recognition in a way that may well never be repeated. Such a claim might appear controversial in our present age of constant, miraculous human and technological self-reinvention, but is nonetheless worthy of argument. A brief outline of what happened during these six hundred years will give an indication.

In Europe the Renaissance would blossom, followed by the Enlightenment and the Industrial Revolution, which in turn ushered in the age of steam, electricity and mechanical engines of all kinds. Spain, having discovered the New World, would reap untold riches in gold and silver from South America, an unearned fortune that would ironically bring about its economic ruin.[31] Meanwhile Portugal, Great

---

31 Oversupply of gold led to inflation and devaluation. Philip II chose to build up an army, borrowing against further gold. When the value and inflow of gold declined – owing to oversupply, piracy and corruption – Philip was forced to default on his debts no less than *four* times during the second half of the sixteenth century. This severely limited Spain's ability to borrow, maintain its army, or even properly run its colonies. The expulsion of the Jews in 1492, with all their financial expertise, had hardly helped matters.

Similar national catastrophes have continued to recur through the ensuing centuries, especially following the sudden discovery of an easily exploitable commodity such as oil. Large quantities of guaranteed income flow directly to various senior government officials, who take their cut on this income. The guaranteed income also helps to keep taxes low, which increases government popularity. However, little money is used, as in direct taxation, for the specific purposes for which it was raised, such as infrastructure maintenance, building up new industries and so forth. Corruption becomes endemic, the economy stagnates, and huge fortunes accrue to the ruling elite.

Britain, France and Holland would each carve out global empires. The wilderness of North America would see the British establish various coastal colonies; owing to inept administration, these colonies would soon cast out their masters. After becoming 'united states', their need for manpower would attract downtrodden emigrants from Europe, until America was on the verge of becoming the world's greatest economy.

During this period (1299–1922), France would become Europe's leading power for four hundred years, undergo an unprecedented Revolution, and then, under Napoleon, set about actually conquering those countries over which it had once merely held sway. All this, and so much more, took place during the long centuries when the Ottoman Empire ruled the Middle East, to a great extent unaffected by what it saw as these external irrelevancies of political and technological transformation.

This is not to imply that the Ottoman Empire remained isolationist. When Mehmed the Conqueror first set eyes on the walls and fortifications of Constantinople, he realised that they were impregnable, even to his army of over 160,000 soldiers. And a siege appeared to be out of the question. The city was built on an isthmus, surrounded by sea on three sides, its coastline protected by high walls. The land side was protected by a three-mile-long double ring of walls, protected by a moat. In all, the walls contained over fifty castles, many with twin towers straddling the few arched gates – the inner ring of walls being 40 feet high and 15 feet thick. Even starvation appeared out of the question, as the inner city contained freshwater wells, as well as gardens for growing produce. It appeared as if a stalemate was inevitable.

But Mehmed the Conqueror had been informed of a Hungarian cannon-founder named Orban, who had boasted that he could make a cannon 'that could blast the walls of Babylon itself'. Mehmed commanded his men to bring Orban to the city of Adrianople, 150 miles to the west, where there was a large iron foundry. Here Orban was ordered to prove that he was as good as his word and build the largest cannon of which he was capable. It took Orban over three months, and the result was a wheeled cannon with a 27-foot muzzle, capable of firing cannon-balls weighing 1,200 pounds over a distance of half a mile.

This monstrous weapon was named 'the basilic' (the king), and it would require sixty oxen to drag it to the walls of Constantinople, where it arrived on 11 April 1453. It was also accompanied by a number of smaller cannons. Mehmed II ordered that the 'basilic' and the other cannons be set up immediately opposite what he calculated was the weakest gate in the walls. He then ordered the cannons to be fired non-stop day in day out.

Orban objected that this would overheat the muzzles of the cannons, which were then liable to disintegrate under the power of their own recoil. Mehmed II was adamant, and a barrage was launched that would last continuously for six weeks. Fortunately, the 'basilic' took three hours to reload, but the smaller cannons proved less resilient, and Orban was killed when one of them exploded. By the end of May, the 'basilic' had opened only a small breach in the outer wall.

By now Mehmed II had lost patience. He ordered his men to charge through the breach in what appeared to be a suicidal assault. At the sight of the Ottoman soldiers, the Byzantines panicked, and tried to flee through a gate in the inner wall. In the midst of the mêlée, the Byzantines omitted to lock the gate behind them. The first Ottomans swarmed into the city itself, followed by wave after wave of their compatriots. The fall of Constantinople on 29 May 1453 is still seen as one of the most significant dates in European history: the ultimate end of any real Roman Empire. The word 'real' is necessary here, for as Voltaire pointed out the so-called Holy Roman Empire, which grew out of Charlemagne's empire, was 'neither Holy, Roman nor an Empire'.[32]

Initially, Venice was the state most affected by this event, as it had previously carried out most of its foreign trade with Constantinople and the eastern Mediterranean, maintaining several strategic ports throughout the Aegean and the Peloponnese. Whilst the rest of Europe remained divided over what action to take, Venice had even sent its own fleet to relieve the siege of Constantinople; though this had barely entered the Aegean before news arrived of the fall of the city. Whereupon, in accordance with the 'pragmatic' policy adopted by Venice during this period, it decided to change sides.

Bartolomeo Marcello, the Venetian ambassador aboard the fleet, was ordered to sail on to Constantinople and negotiate a trade treaty with Mehmed II, choosing to overlook the fact that several hundred Venetians occupying the Venetian trading colony within Constantinople had been put to the sword by the Muslim invaders. Venice justified its change of policy to the rest of Italy by announcing: *Siamo Veneziani, poi Cristiani* – 'We are Venetians, then Christians.'

---

32 Ironically, the Byzantine Empire, which was considered secondary in every sense to the original Roman Empire, lasted twice as long as its illustrious predecessor.

Mehmed II received the new Venetian ambassador Marcello with the contempt he deserved, yet the sultan was also sufficiently versed in statecraft to realise the benefit of maintaining diplomatic relations with Italy's major sea-trading nation. A treaty was signed, and to cement this new accord Venice chose to 'loan' to Mehmed II its greatest artist, Gentile Bellini, who was renowned for the realism and psychological penetration of his portraits. Mehmed II had no truck with the Muslim edict against creating images, and was glad to welcome Bellini to Constantinople. Indeed, despite Bellini's understandable hesitancy, he and Mehmed II soon struck up a firm friendship: 'unique in its intimacy', according to a contemporary observer.

Mehmed II and Gentile both shared a deep interest in the knowledge and history of the Levant, as well as a love of the new sciences that were now beginning to emerge under the inspiration of the Renaissance. Bellini was given full rein to make sketches of life in the newly transformed Constantinople, as well as being commissioned to paint a portrait of Mehmed II himself. This conveys Mehmed seated in half-profile, wearing his large, white sultan's turban, red kaftan and exotic fur shawl. There is no flattery in the depiction of Mehmed's stern features, with their long nose and full brown beard. This is the face of a determined warrior, yet also a man of considerable culture and knowledge.

It was in these last two aspects that the cultural differences between Bellini and Mehmed II would become manifest. Mehmed II asked Bellini to create a painting of St John the Baptist (who was also renowned as a prophet in the Islamic faith). Mehmed II wished Bellini's painting to depict the head of John the Baptist on a platter, when

it was presented to the dancer Salome after she had engin-
eered his beheading.

When Bellini duly presented his meticulously finished
work to Mehmed II, the sultan examined it closely, and
then drew Bellini's attention to a detail in St John's severed
neck. What Bellini had painted was not anatomically
correct. Bellini politely begged to differ; he had, after all,
studied anatomy alongside the young Leonardo da Vinci.
Mehmed II beckoned for his attendants to bring forth a
slave, whom he ordered to be summarily beheaded.
Mehmed then leaned forward, pointing out to the aghast
Bellini the precise error in his painting. Within two years,
Gentile had managed to persuade his friend Mehmed II
to allow him to return to his native Italy.

The Ottomans appear to have originated in the Turkic
heartlands of central Asia, moving west under the banner
of the Mongols. As we have seen, following the split of the
Mongol Empire into four main khanates in the mid-1200s,
Il-Khanate had ruled the south-eastern region of the empire,
occupying Persia and much of Anatolia (modern Turkey).
When Mongol power had waned, this too had disintegrated
into various semi-independent provinces. One of these was
a small tribal territory to the east of the Sea of Marmara,
stretching just over fifty miles long and fifteen miles wide.
This was ruled by Osman I, who had been born in 1254.

Little is known of Osman I's early life, except that he
became ruler of his small territory in 1299, which is usually
taken as the founding date of the Ottoman Empire. Osman
is also known to have had a dream in which 'he saw that
a moon arose from the holy man's breast and came to sink
in his own breast'. When he asked his palace holy man
what this meant, he was told that God had bequeathed the

House of Osman with a great destiny: that it would one day rule over a vast empire with mountains and streams and running waters and gardens. This tale would become a driving myth for Osman and his people, who became known as Ottomans after their ruler. From this time on, Osman I gradually began extending his domain into neighbouring territory ruled by the Byzantine Empire.

Osman I's dream was not only the founding myth of Ottoman national identity, but also played a leading role in the psychology of his descendant Mehmed II, who in 1444 ascended to the sultanate at the tender age of twelve, having scarcely finished his traditional Islamic education at the ancient city of Amasya.[33] Despite being deposed by the Janissaries, the powerful crack troops who formed the sultan's household guard, Mehmed II returned to rule in 1451. It says much of his determination and military skills that within two years he had taken Constantinople, as well as extending his empire's territory well into the Balkans, Anatolia and the northern shores of the Black Sea.

Six years later, Mehmed II would begin building Topkapi Palace, his imperial residence in Constantinople.[34] As imperial palaces go, this speaks volumes for the taste of its

---

33 According to the early Greek geographer, Strabo, this name derives from it once having been the home of the legendary female warriors known as the Amazons.

34 The ancient name, derived from the Roman emperor Constantine the Great, continued to be used. As to a certain extent did the city's even more ancient name Byzantium. Only gradually over the years would the present name Istanbul come into use. There are two conflicting derivations of this name. One claims that Istanbul is a corruption of the Greek phrase '*eis sten polin*' (meaning 'in the city'). However, according to Turkish sources, the name derives from 'Islam bol' (Turkish for 'plenty of Islam').

creator. Here there is none of the dwarfing grandeur of Roman imperial glory, or the overwhelming scale of Versailles. This is an almost homely palace. It is neither imposing from its exterior, nor belittling in its interior. Yet its situation is utterly impregnable. The grounds of the palace and its buildings occupy the narrow foreland that overlooks the Sea of Marmara to the right, the Bosphorus below, and the entrance to the Golden Horn to the left.

The walls that surround it are set at the crest of the steep rocky slopes high above the water, and thus have no need to appear hugely imposing. Inside the main gate, which serves as the entry from the city, the atmosphere is more like that of a university than a palace. Everything is on the human scale, from the comparatively small, well-proportioned buildings to the courtyards and shaded walkways. Fountains play in the gardens. Amidst one courtyard stands a square library building, across another is the modest treasury building.

Behind the walls that encircle the courtyards, there are small pools where the sultan's wives could gather and bathe. And at the far end of the palace, overlooking the vista of the water far below, is a small marble enclave with a single marble seat, where the sultan could sit on his own, gazing down over the vista of the city and the Bosphorus to the shore of Asia.

On the left of the large, second courtyard is the largest building in the palace, the Harem. This housed the sultan's living quarters, as well as those for his wives and concubines. One entrance to this building leads into the Divan, which is lined with the furnishings that now take its name. This was the council chamber where the sultan's Grand Vizier and the other ministers of state would gather on their divans, to hold what were virtually cabinet meetings. High on one wall is a grille, behind which the sultan would sit unseen, watching as his ministers discussed the state business of the day. Afterwards, the sultan was liable to summon any minister to a personal audience, to account for what he had said during the Divan. These debates may have been informal (tea, cakes, or meals could be served), but the manner of discussion was both guarded and discreet. All dreaded a summons to meet the sultan afterwards.

Where wider law was concerned, the Ottomans were a classic example of Kriwaczek's observation concerning the governing of subject people: this was best left as before, but with the new imperial administrators occupying the senior positions. As long as sufficient recruits were inducted into the local imperial army, taxes were gathered, and the annual 'tribute' sent to the Porte (central government administration) in Istanbul, there was little interference from their Ottoman masters. For the most part local courts operated according to local religious custom: Jews were tried by Jewish courts in accord with Talmudic law, Christians had their own courts that applied canon law, and the Muslim courts administered their own version of Sharia law. However, the sultan's decrees were above all laws, and were to be obeyed without question.

There were, of course, exceptions to this pragmatic approach. In a number of conquered territories, the subject people were forcibly converted to Islam, while in others the subject people were 'induced' to convert, with rewards such as lower taxes, access to privileged employment, land ownership and so forth. In this way, many amongst the conquered people were converted. The aftermath of such mixed religious populations remains to this day – accounting for hostilities in such regions as the former Yugoslavia and Cyprus.

Mehmed II may have sought cultural advice from the likes of Venetians such as Bellini; but there is no doubting that the Ottomans were, in many aspects, quite the cultural equal of their European counterparts. Just two years after the conquest of Constantinople, Mehmed II set about building the Grand Bazaar, which remains to this day the largest and finest covered market in the world, containing more than sixty streets and 4,000 shops. At the same time, he embarked upon the Topkapi Palace. Yet the greatest was yet to come.

The Islamisation of Istanbul would reach its apogee under Suleiman the Magnificent, who was born in 1494, just thirteen years after the death of his only rival in greatness, Mehmed the Conqueror. Suleiman would become sultan at the age of twenty-six, and his reign would live up to his epithet. Suleiman was not only the longest serving sultan (forty-six years), but would rule over the Ottoman Empire at its height, expanding his territory until he ruled over 25 million people. (By comparison, the population of the entire continent of Europe during this period was 75 million.)

It was Suleiman the Magnificent who made the inspired choice of Mimar Sinan as his chief architect. Sinan would be responsible for the great and graceful mosques that are such a feature of Istanbul to this day. The Süleymaniye mosque, overlooking the Golden Horn and the Galata Bridge, with its superb squat dome and towering pinnacle minarets, makes an inimitable silhouette against the evening sky. Inside, its gracefully arched courtyard gives way to the ethereal hues, intricate calligraphy, and symmetrical designs of the stained glass windows that adorn the vast, domed interior. This is rightfully judged to be Sinan's finest work in Istanbul. It is certainly a match for Michelangelo's contemporary plans for St Peter's in Rome. Sinan's technique and architectural influence was so great that both the Taj Mahal in India and the tiled modifications of the Dome of the Rock in Jerusalem were heavily inspired by his work.

The Süleymaniye Mosque in Istanbul,
overlooking the entrance to the Golden Horn.

Other influential aspects of Ottoman culture include its cuisine, which would spread from Anatolia throughout the Empire. The variety and ingenuity of its *mezze* (hors d'oeuvres) remain central to restaurant menus all over the eastern Mediterranean. Other ingredients include aubergine, spit-roasted meats, honey-soaked pastries, and all manner of vegetable dishes. Most of these originated as Anatolian or Levantine peasant meals.

Indeed, the transmission of food, and our words to describe it, echo the spread of cultures. As the anthropologist Jared Diamond indicates, the passage from language to language of words describing animals or food often gives surprising insight into the evolution and spread of these items. Consider, for instance, the use of the word describing sheep, indicating the passage of its domestication. Sheep is 'avis' in Sanskrit, 'owis' in Greek, 'ovis' in Latin, 'oveja' in Spanish, 'ovtsa' in Russian, 'avys' in Lithuanian and 'oi' in Irish. English uses the word 'sheep', but the ancient root is preserved in the word 'ewe'.

This leads us to a further historical distinction that can be indicated by language. For example, when William of Normandy took over England in 1066, his army included many French knights, who were rewarded with estates taken from their previous Anglo-Saxon lords. The language spoken at the dinner table was French, while the words used by the lowly servants and cooks remained Anglo-Saxon. Evidence of this remains in the names of animals, and the cooked meat dishes that they provide. Pigs become pork (French: *porc*), sheep becomes mutton (*mouton*), cows become beef (*boeuf*), and so forth.

A host of such deep linguistic divisions between the coloniser and the colonised can be found to this day in the former territories of the Ottoman Empire. Two common examples will suffice. What is called *kebab* in Turkish is insistently named *souvlaki* in Greek. And when asking for a small cup of thick Middle Eastern coffee, one orders Greek coffee in Greece, and Turkish coffee in Turkey.

Another difference in Ottoman culture was noted in 1717 by Lady Mary Montagu, wife of the British ambassador. She observed that the local women of all classes practised 'ingrafting', a process that involved piercing the skin of children with a needle, which had been infected with a tiny amount of smallpox. After a mild bout of smallpox, the child would then be protected from this disfiguring and often fatal disease for life.

At the time, smallpox was one of the greatest medical scourges. According to Voltaire, 60 per cent of the world population were liable to catch this disease, causing a death rate of 20 per cent. The disease was spread via the lungs; and through the centuries none were spared, regardless of class or personal cleanliness. It is now known that Pharaoh Ramesses V had died of this disease as early as the twelfth century BC. Elizabeth I of England had suffered from it, as had Mozart and George Washington. And its effect on the Aztecs would lead to it being described by Dr Edward Jenner as 'the most dreadful scourge of the human species'.

When Lady Mary Montagu returned to England her 'ingrafting' idea was not widely accepted, almost certainly because she was a woman and of no medical qualification. Not until 1796 would Jenner himself introduce the idea of 'ingrafting' with cowpox, rather than smallpox itself. The idea of vaccination was born, and the scourge of smallpox all but eliminated. Few realised, then as now, that this originated from an Ottoman invention.[35]

---

35 In fact, there is evidence that this practice may have been widespread in other parts of Asia, as well as Africa. As early as 1716, the New England puritan minister, Cotton Mather, observed his slave Onesimus administering this procedure. The minister would later put it to good use during an outbreak of smallpox in Boston. Ironically this pioneer scientist was the same Cotton Mather who had previously played a leading role in the Salem witch trials.

By now the Ottoman Empire was at the height of its power, with territory stretching from the Horn of Africa to Algeria. From the time of Suleiman the Magnificent, the Ottomans had virtual control over the whole Mediterranean. This was largely due to a pirate of Albanian descent known as Barbarossa (Red Beard), who had set up his headquarters in Algiers. When the Ottoman army overran the city, it was soon agreed that Barbarossa should remain in charge. This suited both sides. Barbarossa was declared Admiral of the Fleet, and led his considerable naval force to a resounding victory over the combined Christian European navy at Preveza (off western Greece) in 1539.

Algiers would continue as a centre of piracy for centuries to come, attacking ships of all Christian nations. As had happened to Julius Caesar in Ancient Roman times, pirates took important captives hostage, only releasing them from their jail in Algiers when a ransom had been paid. Others were simply sold off as slaves. An indication of the scale of such piracy can be seen from the geographical range of their activities. 'Barbary Pirates', as they became known, seized hostages or slaves from places as far afield as West Africa, Cornwall and Iceland.

Celebrated figures who suffered this fate range from the early Renaissance artist Filippo Lippi (who bought his release by selling skilled portraits of his captors), to the Spanish writer Miguel de Cervantes (who would go on to write *Don Quixote* after his release). But the most renowned of their captives would be the twenty-year-old Aimée de Rivéry, a cousin of Napoleon's wife Josephine, who was taken from a French ship in the Atlantic. The Bey of Algiers quickly realised the high value of such a beautiful white virgin and, in order to gain favour with the Sultan Abdul Hamid I, sent her to Istanbul so that she could be taken into his harem.

It is said that the sultan became so enamoured of Aimée that she was appointed his chief wife, taking on the name Valide Sultan Naksidil. A dominant and well-educated woman, she persuaded her husband to introduce a number of long-overdue reforms, and encouraged close diplomatic ties with France. Doubts have been cast on this story, and although some aspects of it ring hollow, there is no doubting the existence of Valide Sultan Naksidil and her beneficial influence over the sultan.

By the end of the nineteenth century, the power as well as the calibre of the Ottoman sultans had begun to wane. Much of this can be attributed to a uniquely Ottoman tradition known as the *kafes* (cage), which was originally introduced on humanitarian grounds. Prior to the seventeenth century, when the sultan died and his son succeeded, it was the practice for all his brothers to be executed immediately, in order to avoid any sibling claims to the sultanate. Sultan Ahmed I, who acceded to the throne in 1603, decreed an end to this barbaric practice. Instead of having his brother murdered, he had him confined to the *kafes*. Here he was otherwise granted every comfort, including his harem of wives.

This practice would have a number of unintended consequences. When Murad IV died in 1640, he was succeeded by his brother, who became Ibrahim I. By this stage, the new sultan had spent twenty-two years confined in the *kafes*. It is easy to see why he soon became known as Ibrahim the Mad. Utterly ignorant of political practice and protocol, as well as being deprived of the social graces expected of the occupant of the Topkapi Palace, he spent his days frolicking with his harem in the palace pool. When he heard a rumour that one of his wives had been unfaithful to him, he ordered all 280 members of his harem to be tied up in sacks and thrown from a ship into the Bosphorus. According to legend, one of them was rescued by a passing French ship, and ended up living in Paris, where she earned a fortune after her memoirs became a best-seller.

Such degenerate behaviour and erratic decision-making by successive sultans led to a considerable weakening of the Ottoman Empire, and it was now that the European powers began scheming to divide amongst themselves the vast territory of 'the sick old man of Europe'. In 1914, the Ottoman Empire was persuaded to join on the German side in the First World War. By now Turkey and the provinces of its empire were beginning to fall apart. Rumours spread of various groups bidding for power.

The population of Anatolia contained, as it does to this day, a rich blend of nationalities. These were remnants of people who had, over the centuries, conquered or defended the country, as well as people from all over the Ottoman Empire. As such, they included a wide variety of Turkic people (who originated from central Asia), Mongols, Kurds, Armenians – as well as people of Slavic, Caucasian, Greek and Albanian stock.

The notorious Armenian Massacre, which took place in 1915, was provoked by the central government's paranoia concerning this Christian group, or others, taking over the country. In fact, by now most racial groups were partially, if not fully integrated – there were even Armenians who had risen to ministerial level, running such vital institutions as the national mint, the water board and munitions production. Over the coming years of the war, the campaign against the Armenians led to mass deportation and indeed genocide. The very word was coined to describe what had taken place, an event that led to the death of over 1,000,000 people.

In 1918, the Ottoman Empire found itself on the losing side of the war; and at the Treaty of Versailles, Turkey was stripped of its colonial possessions. Consequently, the Greeks launched an opportunistic invasion into the heartland of Anatolia, but were eventually driven back by the skilled General Mustafa Kemal, who had defeated the allies at Gallipoli. In the ensuing confusion, the port city of Smyrna (now Izmir) was burned and as many as 100,000 fleeing Greeks may have lost their lives. A few months later, the last sultan, Mehmed IV, abdicated.

Within months, General Mustafa Kemal took power, naming himself Atatürk ('father of the Turkish people'), and began introducing a widespread programme of reforms intended to 'Europeanise' the supposedly backward country. These included such measures as banning the fez for men, and the veil for women; transposing the Turkish language from Arabic to European script; an attempt to establish parliamentary democracy; as well as abolishing Sharia law and curtailing the power of the religious authorities, especially with regard to education. Almost a century later, disputes have begun to arise once more over most of these reforms, and now it is the Kurds who have become the scapegoats.

Sequence

The Ottoman Empire may be viewed as the last of the old-style empires. As we have seen, initially the world's great empires had usually been initiated by the urge to conquest. (Indeed, in the case of the Mongol Empire, arguably this appears to have been the beginning and the end of the entire project.) Other, more civilising, or more exploitative aspects, came in the wake of conquest.

Yet since the end of the fifteenth century, empire building had undergone a subtle sea change. In both senses of the words: from that time on the sea would play a major role in empire; and change, in the form of historical transformation, or 'advancement', would become a feature excelling even that of Roman times. The Spanish conquest of the New World was almost as domineering as the Mongol Empire, yet in its wake came the extraction of great wealth in the form of gold and silver. The Portuguese, on the other hand, had rounded the Cape of Good Hope in the search of trade. They intended to circumvent the Silk Route to the East, and their success bankrupted the Venetians, the previous main beneficiaries of the trade in valuable oriental spices such as nutmeg, pepper, cinnamon and ginger.[36]

From now on trade would often be the initial inspiration, rather than the secondary consequence, of empire-building. From now on, it would be the age of growing European empires. Europe had become a cockpit of competing nation states. Wars were won and lost, but states survived, more

---

36 Arguably the aim of Columbus was to find a new trade route to Cathay. Similarly, the early conquistadores had been inspired by the myth of El Dorado (The Land of Gold) as much as conquest.

or less intact. No one would conquer the entire continent of Europe until Napoleon. European civilisation advanced, spurred on by such internecine conflicts. In the process, warring European states developed ever more ingenious military inventions, which in turn led to a scientific revolution. (Both Leonardo and Galileo aspired to success as military engineers: Galileo's modified telescope – proposed to the Venetians as a means of advanced warning of any approaching enemy fleet, would only become a revolutionary scientific instrument the moment Galileo raised it to the night sky.)

Meanwhile the rest of the world remained largely untouched by such technical progress, until the Spanish and the Portuguese initiated a new way forward. Other nations on the European landmass soon followed suit. The Dutch, the English, the French . . . all were soon sailing the seven seas in search of trade, with territorial conquest following in its wake. The latter was sometimes prompted by local objections to these interloper traders, but increasingly by the old imperial urge to conquest, in this case prompted more by greed and the wish to keep out other European competitors, rather than the wish to dominate or 'civilise'.

Contrast this with what was happening on the symmetrically opposite side of the Eurasian land mass: China remained undivided and isolated, while its offshore counterpart to Britain (namely Japan), maintained a similar policy of isolation and inwardness. Meanwhile the European nations went on 'discovering' the rest of the world, rapidly claiming its territories as their 'empires'. The greatest of these would become 'the empire on which the sun never set' – namely, the British Empire. This was literally true:

no matter how the globe spun, the sun was always shining on at least one part of this far-flung empire.

On the other hand, it did contain the implicit suggestion that the sun would never set on such an empire. As we have seen, from the outset, this has been a delusion of all great empires. What might be called the Ozymandias syndrome has persisted in the modern era: one of the few reliable lessons of history, its traces can be seen in Hitler's 'Thousand Year Reich' as well as the notion of a permanent 'American hegemony'.

The British Empire

It used to be said that if any power had to dominate the globe during the nineteenth and early twentieth centuries, it might as well have been the British. Other candidates were all lacking in that British sense of fair play and reasonableness. Ironically, it seemed the more 'decent' among the nations in Europe, the more disgraceful were their treatment of their colonies, *viz.* the barbaric rule of the Dutch in the East Indies, and genocide by the Belgians in the Congo.[37]

However, the more one examines this claim mitigating British colonial power, the less clear-cut it becomes. As all were prepared to concede, there had, of course, been a number of blots on British imperial rule. Take the case of India, the so-called 'Jewel in the Crown'.[38] The early nineteenth-century Opium Wars, when the British forced

---

37 Though the Congo was not actually Belgian, but instead was the personal possession of King Leopold II of Belgium, it having been sold to him by the British journalist and explorer Henry Stanley (of 'Dr Livingstone, I presume' fame) after it had been unaccountably turned down by the British.

38 This epithet has its counterpart in reality. The Koh-i-Noor diamond, one of the largest cut diamonds in the world, which originated from India, forms the centrepiece of the actual British crown. The Indian-owned diamond was 'ceded' to Queen Victoria in 1848.

the Chinese to purchase opium grown in India, was hardly 'fair play'. (Consequently 40,000 mainly coastal Chinese became addicts, and China's GDP was halved.)

And then there was the 1919 Amritsar Massacre, sanctioned by the Governor of the Punjab, Michael O'Dwyer, when British soldiers were ordered to open fire on a religious gathering of Sikhs. Official reports were forced to admit up to two hundred deaths. Later investigation revealed that more than 1,000 died and 1,500 were wounded. This single act was said to have been the crystallising moment for the independence movement. Twenty years later, Udam Singh, who had witnessed the massacre, would single-handedly and single-mindedly travel all the way to London, where he would shoot Governor O'Dwyer. After being tried, he would be hanged by the British; to this day his picture is revered in the Golden Temple at Amritsar, the spiritual heart of the Sikh religion.

By this time, the independence movement was being led by Mahatma Gandhi, who would pursue a policy of passive resistance, encouraging his followers to lie down on railway tracks to prevent the passage of trains. With some justification, it has been claimed that such a tactic could only have worked against the British, who threw buckets of sewage over the demonstrators, rather than simply driving the trains over them.

Furthermore, it was the British who had built the railway tracks in the first place, introducing a modern transport system that reached the length and breadth of the subcontinent. This connected cities whose civic buildings were at least the equal of many in Europe, in which British and Indian civil servants ran an administration attempting to 'modernise' a population of hundreds of millions. This involved pursuing a policy of divide and rule, incentives, indigenous military recruitment and selective threat of force. To give an idea of the magnitude of this task: in 1900, 165,000 British (administrators and army) ruled over around 330 million Indians.

The British administration (often aided by the army) would introduce modern irrigation, forestry, a new legal system (and new prisons), as well as widespread education (in English). They would look on in bemusement as the Indians founded their own steel industry, which saw the rise of Tata Steel, now one of the world's largest companies. Yet at the same time, for over 150 years, India's GDP would remain stagnant – some even claim that it halved. Meanwhile the GDP of Great Britain increased by nearly 700 per cent during this same period, much of this due to British imports from India, such as jute, cotton, spices and even rice (despite famines).

On the other hand, enlightened policies led to the growth of a thriving Indian middle class, a few even educated at prestigious English public schools. It was intellectuals from this emergent class who would one day form the backbone of the independence movement.[39] Once again we come up against the perennial double-edged question, 'What have the Romans ever done for us?' Which also begs the question: 'What have the Romans done *to* us?'

In keeping with the new European empires, the British Empire began as exploration with a view to trade. As early

---

39 Nehru, India's first prime minister went to Harrow and Cambridge. Jinnah (the first prime minister of Pakistan) and Gandhi both studied law and became barristers in London.

as 1497, the Venetian Zuan Cabotto (anglicised to John Cabot) was financed by a group of Bristol merchants to sail west across the Atlantic, in the wake of Columbus. Ironically, Cabot made landfall near where the Vikings had established their brief Vinland colony some 500 years earlier, a place which Cabot named 'New Found Launde'. Cabot was under the misapprehension that he had landed in China, and decided against founding a colony.

Almost a century later, in 1585, Sir Walter Raleigh established a colony at Roanoke island in Virginia, which was then the English name for the entire coast north of the Spanish-claimed territory of Florida. It was from Virginia that Raleigh first brought potatoes and tobacco back to England. But when a British ship arrived at Roanoke in 1590, it was found that all the inhabitants had mysteriously vanished. In 1607, the British would establish the first permanent settlement in the Americas at Jamestown, some 100 miles north of 'The Lost Colony' of Roanoke.

Just half a century earlier, the English sailor John Hawkins had hijacked a Portugese ship sailing from Africa to the Caribbean carrying 301 black slaves, which he sold at Santo Domingo. Finding this to be a lucrative business, he then embarked upon the 'triangular' slave trade, which was already being operated by several European nations. This involved a ship sailing from Europe with a cargo of textiles, various tools, weapons and rum. On arrival in West Africa, these cheap European manufactured goods would be sold to local chieftains in return for slaves.

The ship then embarked upon the second leg of the triangle, the notorious 'middle passage' across the Atlantic, for the Caribbean. The cargo of chained black slaves were laid out below decks in closely packed rows, where they endured stifling heat and appalling conditions. Many died, though it was in the interests of the captain, as well as the profit of his backers, to ensure that as many as possible amongst this precious cargo remained alive.

Ships carrying 250 slaves (sometimes even 600) would transport their human cargo in this fashion to the West Indies, where they were sold to the owners of sugar plantations. The slaves were then set to the backbreaking task of hacking down sugar canes in the sub-tropical heat. Some slaves were sold as far north as the British plantations in Virginia.

The first Africans arrived in the British colony of Jamestown as early as 1619. These were said to be 'indentured labour', rather than 'permanent' slaves. That is, they were bound to work for their masters as slaves for a fixed period, whereupon they were released, and sometimes given a plot of land. By 1619, there were also a number of English indentured labourers serving at Jamestown. These were men (and women) who had been found guilty of crimes in their homeland and sentenced to a period of indentured labour in the overseas 'plantations'.

Jamestown was thus not only a plantation colony, producing cotton, tobacco, and wood for export, but also a penal colony using convicts as a form of quasi-slave labour. In 1640, one black and two white indentured labourers escaped from Jamestown and fled north towards Maryland. All three were soon recaptured, and brought before the Virginia Governor's Council. The two white fugitives were sentenced to serve out longer indentures, while the black fugitive, named John Punch, was sentenced to permanent (i.e. lifelong) indenture. In the words of

Radney Coates of Miami University, this made John Punch 'the first official slave in the English colonies'.[40]

The slave trade was carried out by almost all European maritime nations, even Sweden and Russia. It is reliably estimated to have transported up to 12.5 million Africans across the Atlantic, with some 10.7 million surviving the Middle Passage, before slavery was abolished. The British campaigner, William Wilberforce, finally managed to get an act through parliament abolishing the trafficking of slaves in 1807, with the United States following suit in 1808. Consequently, a British naval squadron was tasked with intercepting slave ships leaving west Africa.

Even so, slavery would continue until 1833 in the sugar plantations of the British Caribbean, after which the sugar plantation owners forced to free their slaves received 'compensation for loss of property' of around £20 million in total.[41] This sum represented no less than 40 per cent of the British government's annual expenditure (navy, army, civil administration and authority throughout the land, and so on). In present terms, this payout would be worth around £16.5 billion.

Despite the efforts of Wilberforce and the British navy, the slave trade represents more than a mere blot on the reputation of the British Empire. It has been argued in mitigation that all the other major powers were involved, and the British were the first to abolish it altogether. (The United States did not abolish internal slavery until 1865,

---

40 Astonishingly, recent DNA analysis has revealed that John Punch was the twelfth-generation grandfather of Barack Obama on his *mother's* side.

41 No one appears to have considered the slaves themselves worthy of compensation.

while in Brazil it persisted until 1888.) Indeed, all previous empires we have discussed relied heavily upon slavery. From their everyday life to their great monuments: from the pyramids to the graceful columns of the Parthenon, from the immense cavern dug out to house Emperor Huang's terracotta army, and the stones hewed and hauled to construct the great mosques of Istanbul . . . all were only made possible using massive quantities of slave labour. But this was the distant past.

Perhaps our main concern with slavery in the British Empire (as well as in the Americas and other European empires) is that the proceeds from this unspeakable trade laid the foundations of the modern world we inhabit today. The vast influx of money from the sugar plantations built great fortunes in Britain. Nick Draper of UCL, who has made a revealing study of the compensation received by British slave owners, estimates 'as many as one-fifth of wealthy Victorian Britons derived all or part of their fortunes from the slave economy'.

In fact, by 1833 there were over 46,000 British owners of slaves. This was how the ancestors of George Orwell, Graham Greene, ex-PM David Cameron, and a host of others made their fortunes; even the Bishop of Exeter received over £4,000 (presently worth around half a million pounds). And perhaps more surprisingly, half of the beneficiaries of the 1833 compensation were women, who had for the most part received ownership of their slaves through family inheritance.

This was the wealth that would create banks, country mansions and vast estates. It would also fund the age of steam, of canals, of railways and the world's greatest navy. This was the money that financed the Industrial Revolution, which made Britain and its empire into the greatest power in the world. An Industrial Revolution that spread and transformed Europe. An Industrial Revolution that spread modernity across the globe. In other words, the world as we know it is built on this money. As Balzac observed: 'Behind every great fortune there is a great crime.'

Passing to the other side of the world and the eastern origins of the British Empire, one of its earliest and most significant territories was a tiny island less than two miles long and half a mile wide, in what is now Indonesia. This was the island of Run, in the Banda Islands, which lie amidst the various scattered archipelago that occupy the 800 miles of sea between what are now known as Borneo and Papua New Guinea. The Banda Islands had originally been 'discovered' by the Portuguese in 1511. Then in 1609, the Dutch East India company muscled in. But in 1611, the British captain, Nathaniel Courthorpe, took possession of the island of Run.

The attraction of this obscure archipelago was that these islands were at the time the world's sole source of nutmeg and mace, two spices which were so highly prized in Europe that they were worth more than their weight in gold. Besides being highly prized as a condiment, nutmeg was also valued for its alleged medicinal properties – believed to be capable of curing everything from the 'bloody flux' to the plague. Ten pounds of nutmeg could be purchased in Run for just one English penny (old style). Back in London, this could be sold for the equivalent of £2.50; some goods had a mark-up of as much as 68,000 per cent.

After the British laid claim to Run, the Dutch sporadically laid siege to the island. The British maintained a tenuous hold on the island until a few years before 1677, when a peace treaty was signed with the Dutch at Breda, in Holland. Under the terms of this treaty, Britain agreed to relinquish all claim to Run in exchange for a slightly larger island held by the Dutch in the Americas, namely Manhattan Island. Whereupon, the local settlement of New Amsterdam (population 2,500) was renamed New York.

According to historian Giles Milton, the trade in oriental spices such as nutmeg, pepper, ginger and cinnamon, would bring about 'a new age of revolutionary economics based on credit, the rise of a rudimentary banking system and ultimately free enterprise.' Here was the beginning of modern capitalism. The epitome of this revolution can be seen in the rise of the joint stock company – most notably the English East India Company. This was granted a royal charter in 1600 by Queen Elizabeth I, giving the company a monopoly on English trade with the East for fifteen years.

This allowed a group of London merchants to buy 'shares' in the company, which would then be run by a board of directors. The capital accumulated from the sale of these shares allowed the directors to purchase a ship, man it and load it with cargo; giving the captain instructions to sail around the Cape of Good Hope, and trade its cargo for valuable spices in the East Indies (at the time a vague appellation covering the whole of India, south-east Asia and even China). When (or if) the ship successfully returned to England, its cargo of spices would be sold, with the shareholders benefitting from the profits according to their 'share' of the total initial investment.

Financial innovation, involving credit, free enterprise and 'rudimentary' banking were very much in the air during this period. The Dutch led the way with the largest stock exchange in Europe at Amsterdam. Even so, it would not be until 1602 that the Dutch founded their own Dutch East India Company, which would seek to monopolise the spice trade in what became known as the Dutch East Indies (modern Indonesia). Other Europeans, such as the Portuguese and even the Danes, were already running similar schemes, but the English and Dutch East India Companies would soon emerge as the major players, with what would become the British East India Company virtually taking over the whole of India within two hundred years.

The profits accruing to the British East India Company were soon greater than those of the West Indies sugar plantations. Competition with the Dutch and French companies quickly led to armed skirmishes. By 1800, the British East India Company was a state within a state. It appointed its own governors of India. It had its own navy, consisting of both merchant and armed vessels. Its armed navy was even able to conduct its own wars, such as the Opium Wars against China. The company also ran its own army of 260,000 men, with British officers commanding locally recruited soldiers. This was twice the size of the entire British Army (official version), and was used for conducting campaigns against independent maharajahs. The defeat in 1799 of the fearsome Tippu Sahib, Sultan of Mysore, saw Arthur Wellesley (later to become Duke of Wellington) notch up his first victory.

Then in 1857 came the Indian Mutiny, which began in Delhi and soon spread throughout central India. Although this was eventually put down, with much savagery on both sides, the British government back in London had had enough. The British Empire was no place for an entire sub-continent to be ruled by an independent commercial enterprise, and the government nationalised the East India Company. India was placed under British colonial rule and a few years later Queen Victoria would be declared Empress of India.

By now the British Empire had expanded to truly global proportions. In 1759, General Wolfe and his soldiers scaled the cliffs at Quebec on the St Lawrence River, and took the French city. Four years later, Canada became a British colony. However, ten years after that, when the British government imposed taxes on the American colonies, and then tried to sell them tea (imported tax free by the East India Company from China), this resulted in the Boston Tea Party. Colonists dressed as Native Americans boarded the ships and cast tea chests into Boston harbour. Demonstrations against inept British rule, under the slogan 'No taxation without representation', soon spread throughout the thirteen British colonies in America, and in 1776 they achieved a historic victory, forming the United States of America.

By now Captain Cook had sailed the south Pacific and planted the British flag in Australia, claiming the entire territory for the Empire in 1770. After the British had lost their American colonies, they no longer had a penal colony where they could exile such criminals as were deemed not worthy of hanging. The theft of a sheep, or 'goods valued at twelve pence', merited the death penalty; pickpockets and juvenile offenders were merely exiled for life to penal colonies in the Americas, where they usually worked as indentured labourers. But now that Australia had been discovered, the authorities decided that this was just the place to establish a new penal colony, and in 1788 a ship carrying the first prisoners arrived at Botany Bay (now Sydney).

The empire may have been flourishing across the globe,

but the majority of the people back home, like those who had been subjugated abroad, derived little benefit from this. On the contrary, the Industrial Revolution resulted in an exodus from rural areas to the cities in search of work. What they found was even worse than the servitude of working the land. The rapidly expanding cities were soon teeming with factory workers enduring long hours and housed in appalling conditions. The figures speak for themselves. In 1700, Manchester had been a small market town with a population of 10,000. By 1800, this had become 95,000; by 1850 it had become 250,000.

When the German factory owner, Friedrich Engels, moved to Manchester and saw for himself the unbelievable squalor of the slums, he wrote to his friend Karl Marx, and together they composed the Communist Manifesto, with its stirring call to arms: 'Workers of the world unite!' The British Empire was making people rich, but throughout the world, and even at home, the condition of its subjects was often a humanitarian disgrace. (The fact that the Marxist system simply doesn't work, and itself would often lead to conditions of widespread and appalling distress when it was applied, does in no way gainsay the disgraceful conditions it sought to alleviate.)

When the First World War broke out in 1914, many thousands of young men in cities throughout Britain enthusiastically volunteered to join the army. The army's slogan was, 'Britain Needs You'. The slogan of many joining up was: 'This is our chance to get out of here, lads.' Three years later, word spread through the trenches that there had been a revolution in Russia, and many of those same lads rejoiced at the news that somewhere at last all men might be equal. Years later, when my father had become a successful businessman in London, he was in the habit of raising his glass, 'To the Kaiser and Lenin.' When the bemused company would ask what he meant by this seemingly contradictory toast, he would reply: 'The Kaiser got me out of Glasgow, and Lenin made me believe there could be justice on this earth.'

Ironically, the British Empire had always had trouble at home. It had taken centuries for the component territories of Great Britain to acquiesce to what was for the most part English domination. In 1301, after Edward I had defeated the Welsh, he promised them 'a prince born in Wales who did not speak a word of English'. The Welsh assumed that this would be a Welshman who spoke the Welsh language, but they had been tricked. Their new prince turned out to be Edward I's infant son, who happened to have been born in the (English) castle at Caernarvon in Wales. From this time on, the reigning monarch's son has traditionally taken the title Prince of Wales.

The Scots proved more troublesome, bitterly contesting all attempts at conquest by the 'auld enemy'. Then came the last years of the seventeenth century, when the Scots decided to branch out into the empire business, attempting to found a colony of their own at Darien, in Panama. This was financed by the Company of Scotland, a joint-stock company on the East India Company model. (Ironically, this Scottish company was founded by William Paterson, the Scotsman who had successfully founded the Bank of England.) Everyone in Scotland became enthused with this patriotic scheme, and all who could sank their savings into it.

When the so-called Darien Scheme failed – largely due to its ill-chosen jungle site, and its vulnerability to Spanish attack – the entire nation was bankrupted. In 1707, Scotland signed an Act of Union with England, prompting the national poet Rabbie Burns to declare that the Scots 'were bought and sold for English gold'. There followed unsuccessful rebellions in 1715 and 1745. In the latter, the Scots reached Derby, just over 100 miles short of London, but when no one turned up to fight them, they simply returned home.

The third of England's Celtic neighbours, the Irish, suffered worst of all. The Normans had invaded as early as 1169. After the Reformation, England's fear of Catholic Ireland being used as a base for European Catholic powers to attack mainly Protestant England, led to further incursions and rebellions. Through the sixteenth and seventeenth centuries, 'plantations' were established, during which the indigenous Irish were driven off land that was then given to Protestant immigrants, largely from Scotland. These occupied much of the north of the country. Famine and emigration cut a swathe through the entire country during the nineteenth century. By 1841, the population of Ireland had risen to 8.5 million. By 1900 this had fallen to 4.5 million.

Then in 1916, an uprising was staged in Dublin, which was partly put down by shells lobbed into the city by a British naval vessel at the mouth of the River Liffey. Many view this as the first people's revolution of the twentieth century (coming, as it did, just a year prior to the Bolshevik Revolution in Russia). In 1922, Ireland would finally gain independence. The country which had a claim to being the first colony of the British Empire, was now the first colony to break free from it. (America didn't count. As far as the Irish were concerned, this was just a civil war amongst the English. And besides, by now large sections of New York, Boston and Chicago had been colonised by the Irish.)

A map of the British Empire at its greatest extent (1921).

By 1913, the 'Dark Continent' of Africa had been all but totally divided between the European powers. Only Liberia and Ethiopia remained free, with the British and the French taking the lion's share. Cecil Rhodes, the British imperialist par excellence, had pushed north from the Cape Colony with the aim of founding British colonies 'from the Cape to Cairo', but was temporarily thwarted by the German colonisation of Tanganyika (now mainland Tanzania).

The success and retention of the British Empire depended largely upon the British navy. Being an island race, the British had long understood that their only defence against more powerful continental neighbours lay in 'ruling the waves'. When the occasion arose, it was the British navy that had guaranteed British sovereignty. By defeating the Spanish Armada in 1588, Drake had 'singed the King of Spain's beard'. Nelson's victory over the French fleet at Trafalgar in 1805 ensured that Napoleon could not launch an invasion. The Royal Navy didn't actually win the Battle of Jutland against the Germans in 1916 – if anything, it was a draw, with the Germans claiming to have inflicted greater losses. But after this confrontation, the Germans had no alternative but to return to port, where they remained confined for the rest of the war. Not for nothing is the navy known in Britain as the 'Senior Service'. However, it was the junior service, the upstart Royal Air Force, who in 1940 won the Battle of Britain in the skies over southern England, once again ensuring that no invasion could be launched.

So how did the British Empire end? By 1914, the European powers had taken over almost the entire globe – with the British, the French, the Dutch, the Spanish and the Portuguese leading the way. Germany, by now the powerhouse of central Europe, had been a latecomer – for the simple reason that Bismarck's united German Reich had only come into existence in 1871, too late to pick up anything but a few bits and pieces of unconquered territory that lay scattered across the globe. So, what next? Perhaps inevitably – despite a 'foolproof' network of interlocking alliances – the Europeans turned on each other, tearing apart their continent in what became known as the First World War.

The Western allies, led by Britain and France, were only rescued by the Americans, after which US President Wilson presided over the Versailles Peace Conference. His message was self-determination for all peoples. This was accepted in Europe, but the superior diplomatic skills of the British and the French ensured that no such enlightened policy was applied to empires outside Europe. The British Empire was safe, but in fighting the war the British themselves had run up huge debts with the Americans.

Just over twenty years later, Europe once again began

tearing itself apart. On this occasion the Americans arrived a little earlier, just in time to save solitary Britain (and the distant USSR) holding out against Hitler. After this war, Britain was indebted to America to the tune of £21 billion (a debt that would not finally be paid off until 2006). In 1945, Britain could barely support itself, let alone an empire. The largest 'white colonies', such as Canada, South Africa and Australia, had already been granted 'dominion status' (virtual, then increasingly real, independence). By now the message of self-determination had spread across the globe.

Reluctantly, Britain was forced to grant independence to India in 1948. One by one, over the coming decades, the British colonies struggled to follow suit. Armed conflict was tempered by negotiations with leaders of independence movements. (It became almost a rite of passage for the future leader of a newly independent nation to have served time in a British jail.) Finally, only a few tiny outposts remained. These were either unwilling to pay, or could not afford, the expenses involved in independence – or were possessed of a British patriotism that had long since vanished in the motherland.

These last remnants now include only the likes of Gibraltar, the Falkland Islands, and St Helena (once Napoleon's own personal penal colony). Meanwhile there remain some scattered island 'protectorates' in the Indian and Pacific Oceans – ensuring that the sun still never sets on the British Empire, but only just, and only in the most literal sense.

The next empire runs almost parallel to the British Empire, but only in temporal terms. Any other comparison of the two provides an object lesson in the vagaries of sideways history.

9

The Russian Empire

Churchill famously described Russia as 'a riddle, wrapped in a mystery, inside an enigma'. This was the case for centuries before Churchill made his remark, and indeed arguably remains so to this day. What will Russia do next? What will become of Russia?

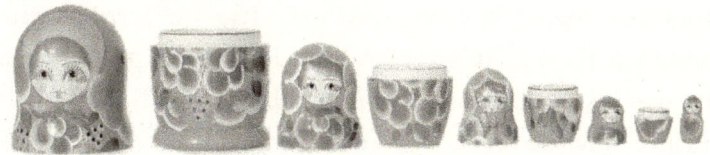

A series of Russian Nesting Dolls, each of which fits inside the other (from right to left).

The fact that so much of Russia is still opaque, even in the age of internet technology and social media, remains an enigma in itself. This undeniably has something to do with its sheer size and the variety of its people. Russia is far and away the largest country in the world. In its present state it covers over 6.6 million square miles. (Canada comes a poor second, with 3.8 million square miles.) Then there is the question of national pride, and an accompanying mistrust of foreign influences, which encourages an element of secretiveness.

Geographically speaking, all of Russia west of the Ural Mountains is part of Europe. Yet culturally speaking Russia has always remained ambivalent about its European status. Three hundred years ago, Peter the Great founded St Petersburg on the marshy shores of the Baltic. This was intended to be Russia's 'Window to the West' – a new city of classical stone facades to replace the age-old 'wooden' Moscow as the capital. Russia had begun to modernise, but this Europeanisation was never fully accepted, even amongst the nobility. Arguably, the heart of old Russia remained in Moscow, with its walled Kremlin of ancient cathedrals, onion-domed towers and palaces.[42]

The Russian Empire began as it meant to go on. Its founder is generally recognised to be Ivan the Terrible, who assumed the title 'Czar of All the Russias' in 1547, when he was just seventeen. His grandfather Ivan III, the Grand Prince of Moscow, had driven the remnants of the Mongols/ Tatars from central Muscovy at the end of the previous century, expanding his domain north-west to the shores of the Baltic and north-east to the shores of the Arctic Ocean.

Ivan the Terrible's childhood was copybook psychopath. He ascended to the princedom of Muscovy at the age of three, after his father died from blood-poisoning. His

---

42 The word Kremlin literally means 'fortress inside a city'. Each ancient city of Russia had a Kremlin at its centre, much as ancient Greek cities, and indeed cities throughout the Middle East, have their ancient acropolis, or citadel.

mother would die five years later, from a more direct form of poisoning by a palace faction. This left young Ivan to be groomed by rival groups of Boyars. These were the feudal aristocrats of Eastern Europe, their name deriving from the old Bulgarian word *boylare*, meaning 'noble'. While Muscovy was plunged into chaos by rival boyars, the young Ivan grew up amidst a court filled with intrigue, suspicion and poisoning. His response was to develop a habit of torturing small animals.

Despite such an unpropitious upbringing, Ivan grew into an intelligent young man, well-versed in literature and music. He also developed an ambition to restore the country back to the pre-Mongol days of the earlier Kievan Rus' federation, when the principalities and domains occupied by the Rus' stretched from the Baltic to the Black Sea and east towards the Ural Mountains. To a large extent this had grown from the hinterland of the Daugava-Dnieper River systems down which the original Vikings had sailed from Scandinavia to the Black Sea and Constantinople in the tenth century.

It was this link with Constantinople that had been responsible for the population of Rus' becoming Christians. Vladimir the Great, the ruler of Kievan Rus' in the early eleventh century, was a convinced pagan, worshipping the ancient Viking and Slavic gods. In common with the prevailing practices expected of a pagan ruler, he took several wives and some eight hundred concubines. He appeased the gods for his continuing good fortune by erecting many shrines and statues to them.

For some time, Christian missionaries had ventured from Constantinople into Kievan Rus', suffering much martyrdom in the process. However, these 'Apostles to the Slavs' would introduce a number of beneficial innovations. They set down the oldest known version of the slavic alphabet, the Glagolitic alphabet, which was modelled on the Greek alphabet. Their followers would later go on to develop the Cyrillic script, named after the Byzantine St Cyril, who had pioneered the earlier slavic alphabet. In time, Cyrillic would come to be used by the Russian, Eastern European and North Asian languages.

Vladimir was so impressed by the advances introduced by these Christian monks that he began to have his doubts about the pagan gods, and dispatched commissioners to study other religions, such as Judaism, Islam, Roman Catholicism and Byzantine Orthodox Christianity. The commissioners dispatched by Vladimir to Constantinople were overwhelmed by the beauty of a service conducted in the huge domed cathedral of Hagia Sophia, the finest building in the Byzantine world. 'We no longer knew whether we were in heaven or on earth,' they told Vladimir.

Consequently, Vladimir was baptised in 987. He then summoned the entire population of Kiev to gather in the waters of the River Dnieper, where they were given a mass baptism. From now on, Kievan Rus' would be a Christian nation. Surprisingly, the people of Kievan Rus' took to the new religion and a strong connection was made to Byzantium. This would even outlast the centuries of Mongol rule (1237–1480). Yet the Mongol conquest would have the effect of isolating still further the people of Rus' from Europe, an isolation that would persist even after the Mongols had been driven out by Ivan the Terrible's grandfather.

When Ivan had himself crowned 'Czar of all the Russias', this was more than an act of self-aggrandisement, it also harked back symbolically to a past that was by now all but legendary. Ivan was claiming the legacy of the pre-Mongol Kievan Rus'. According to the contemporary US historian Janet Martin, a specialist in medieval Russia: 'The new title symbolised an assumption of powers equivalent and parallel to those held by the former Byzantine caesar and the Tatar khan, both known in Russian sources as Czar. The political effect was to elevate Ivan's position.' The Czar was thus not only the secular ruler of Russia, but also its divine leader, who had been appointed by God to enact his will.

The concept of the 'Divine Right of Kings' was widely accepted in Europe, too. On the other hand, the ultimate religious power remained universal and separate, in the form of the Pope. And even here, religious power would not remain absolute. In the early years of the sixteenth century, western Europe would be split by the Reformation. The century preceding this had seen the Renaissance, which affected Europe's entire culture. Art, architecture, literature and science would all be transformed under the influence of a new humanism, derived ultimately from Ancient Greek and Roman sources. This philosophy placed a crucial value on individual humanity, creating a profound mental sea change.

The medieval world, which saw this life as merely a preparation for the day of judgement and the life to come, was drained of its psychological imperative. All this change – a fundamental shift in Western civilisation – was taking place in a Europe that had little contact with Russia. Even the connection to Constantinople had been broken, when the Byzantine world was swept away by the Ottomans.

From 1547 on, the Russians would be ruled by a Czar who had absolute secular and spiritual power. And all the while the country would remain in isolation. Decisive developments in European history – from the Magna Carta (the first guarantee of civil rights), to the Renaissance and the Reformation (which saw the Protestants split from the Roman Catholic church),[43] would see no echo in Russia.

However, when Europe tore itself apart in the brutal, mainly religious Thirty Years War (1618–1648), this had been preceded in Russia during the reign of Feodor I (Ivan the Terrible's son) by the 'Time of Troubles' (1606–1613). The latter witnessed a similarly widespread catastrophe to that which would affect central Europe. Though indicatively it was not prompted by religious division. A corrupt Czardom and ineffective administration was tipped into anarchy following the cold summers of 1601–1603, when ruined crops unleashed famine and uprisings.

In the West, Polish-Lithuanian forces took advantage of this chaos to invade Russia, even taking Moscow in 1610. But, as Napoleon and Hitler would later discover, reaching Moscow was no guarantee of victory over Russia. The wooden city was set on fire, and a patriotic, largely 'volunteer' army forced the invaders to withdraw in 1612.

These volunteers would not have volunteered of their own accord; they would largely have consisted of serfs, who had been 'volunteered' by their feudal owners. Serfdom in Russia meant that the landed gentry legally owned the peasants who worked on their land. Serfdom had largely died out in western Europe with the collapse of the feudal

---

43 This signalled a fundamental shift in the nature of the Christian faith. From now on, individual Protestant worshippers could pray directly to God, without the intermediary of a priest (or Czar).

system, which never fully recovered after the Black Death. In Russia, serfdom would not be abolished until 1861 (i.e. four years *before* slavery was abolished in the Deep South of the United States). Following the chaos of the 'Time of Troubles', in 1613 an assembly of feudal lords voted for the installation of a new dynasty of Czars – namely, the Romanovs. The first of the new line of Romanov Czars would be Michael I, whose grandfather had been adviser to Ivan the Terrible, as well as being a brother of his first wife, the Czarina Anastasia.

It was during the rule of Michael I that Russia began its more lasting expansion beyond the Urals into Siberia. By 1639, Russian explorers had reached the Pacific Ocean, with a settlement being established in 1647 at Okhotsk, which lies some 1,200 miles north of modern-day Vladivostok. (An indication of the sheer scale of Russia can be seen from the fact that Okhotsk is 3,500 miles east of Moscow, with the easternmost point of Russia being a further 1,500 miles away.)

The Khanate of Sibir, a region of indigenous tribes and diverse Muslim peoples had officially been a vassal state of Russia since 1555. Yet not until the following century would the region known as Siberia become part of the Russian Empire. Cossacks defeated the local tribes, establishing forts. The Russian state then collected taxes from the subdued tribespeople, allegedly in exchange for protection from their long-term enemies – further tribespeople who had not yet been subdued. Meanwhile other Cossacks conducted expeditions to collect the fur of sables, foxes and ermines, which fetched a high price in western Russia and even more in the markets of western Europe.

The furthest north-eastern regions of Siberia were

occupied by tribes of the Koryak people and the Chutki, many of whom had been isolated from outer contact since Stone Age times. The fierce climate had ensured that these remote nomadic peoples remained at a stage of development that had vanished from Europe around 4,000 years previously. Siberia became Russia's 'Wild East', which existed as such some two centuries prior to the American 'Wild West'. But whereas the latter consisted of expansive plains and would be settled by pioneer farmers and 'cowboys', the very different terrain of forests and tundra in the Wild East was settled mainly by escaped prisoners, fugitive serfs and 'Old Believers'.

These last were Orthodox Christians, who rejected the reforms introduced in an attempt to align the Russian Orthodox Church more closely with its Greek Orthodox parent. These liturgical and ritual reforms had been instigated in 1666–67 by Patriarch Nikon of Moscow, under the auspices of Czar Alexis, the son of Michael I. From this time on, all who clung to the ancient rites were anathematised, or placed under the curse of God. This meant that they could only continue to practise their faith in regions beyond European Russia and the Urals.

Owing to the nature of Siberia and the spread of its new inhabitants, even its remotest outposts were viewed as part of an expanding Russian Empire, rather than as distinct colonies. This eastward expansion continued to such an extent that just 100 years after the reaching of the Pacific, the Danish explorer Vitus Bering, in the employ of the Russian navy, ventured into the strait named after him. From here he spotted the distant shoreline of continental America, making landfall and claiming the territory in the name of the Czar. Trappers and hunters would soon follow, establishing themselves in Alaska and eventually pushing many hundreds of miles down the archipelago of the western American seaboard.

The liturgical reforms of 1666–67 were a rare attempt to unify Russia with its European neighbours. Unfortunately, this unity was achieved with the Orthodox religion, which now flourished only in the more backward parts of southern Europe, as well as the Levant and beyond. These areas had been barely touched by the great developments taking place in northern and western Europe, such as the Renaissance and the Reformation. Just a year after the Russians implemented their religious reforms, the disastrous Thirty Years War that had devastated western central Europe came to an end. But with the cessation of hostilities came a transformation of Western political thought, which remains to this day.

The 1668 Treaty of Westphalia laid the foundations of international politics. It established the idea of national self-determination, the sovereignty of the state, and decreed against any involvement in national affairs by neighbouring states. Nations existing side by side with different customs, culture, religion or race were not to interfere with each other, no matter how antithetical such practices might be.

As far as European nations have been concerned, this principle may have been honoured as much in the breach as in the observance over the centuries since 1668. However, the seed was sown. The prolonged preliminary negotiations for the Treaty of Westphalia were attended, on and off, by 194 different states (many little more than German family dukedoms). All signed up to the new order, which has remained central to international law. Ironically, although the European powers would practise no such observance

in the establishment of their world-wide empires, this principle would be a major argument for the peoples seeking
liberation from these empires, and especially in the creation
of the United Nations.

In the immediate aftermath of the Treaty of Westphalia,
Switzerland would be granted freedom from Austria, and
the Netherlands from Spain. Russia did not attend these
negotiations, and indeed throughout its long history the policy
of the Russian Empire – in its various forms – has seldom
paid regard to this notion of national self-determination.
Further irony emerges in the fact that during this very
period Russia would be ruled by Peter the Great, the Czar
who did his utmost to drag Russia into the European sphere
of enlightenment and modernity. His forty-three-year rule,
from 1672 until 1725, would transform the country from
a state of historical stasis into a major European power
and participant in the continent's affairs.

From the outset, Peter was different. His father, Alexis I,
ensured that he had the best available education. This
involved being taught by a variety of tutors, including an
aristocratic Scottish soldier of fortune, who believed in
'making outdoor games with live ammunition'. At the age
of ten, Peter was chosen to be Czar by the Boyar Duma
(a council of noblemen). After a period of family squabbles,
Peter finally became a fully independent ruler at the age
of twenty-two. By now he had sprouted to the exceptional
height of six foot eight inches, but his frame was weak and
he suffered from facial tics.

Even at this early age, Peter already had in mind a grand
plan for Russia. This can be summed up in one word:
Reform. He wished to transform the country from top to
bottom, turning Russia into a state on the European model.

His reign started with an edict banning beards and robes from his court, commanding that European dress would be worn from now onwards.

The young new Czar Peter then set off with a large delegation to form alliances with European monarchs and discover for himself how the modern world worked. He insisted upon travelling incognito, but this soon descended into farce owing to his towering height and his outrage when members of his delegation omitted to treat him with the exaggerated deference expected of all citizens in the presence of the Czar. Peter's extended tour of Europe included longer stays in France, England and Holland, where he observed and learned a great deal regarding the achievements of Western civilisation. Europe was entering the Age of the Enlightenment, which placed a premium on rational thought and scientific advancement – a total contrast to the mystical thought so prevalent in Russia.

This early Russian incursion into Europe would also bring lasting diplomatic results. Eventually treaties would be signed with Venice and the Holy Roman Empire, which guarded Russia's southern flanks from the Ottoman Empire; and a treaty with Denmark opened the way to the Baltic without Swedish interference. The latter would result in Peter's greatest undertaking, the building of St Petersburg. This would guarantee Russia a port giving access to Europe for almost the entire year. Its only other northern port, Archangel, was iced up for months on end during the long winters.

Although this new city was named in honour of Peter's patron saint, indicatively it was given the German suffix 'burg'. In the new Czar's eyes, Germany stood for all things modern. Swiss, French and Scots architects were imported, and a vast army of peasants was press-ganged in from all over the country. These drained the marches and constructed the grand buildings that lined the grid of canals on Vasilyevsky island, the central island at the mouth of the Neva. The project had been started in 1703, when the Swedes had been driven from their fortress at the mouth of the Neva, and in 1712 Peter the Great (as he was now becoming known) transferred the capital to St Petersburg. During the course of building the city, many tens of thousands of peasants would lose their lives.

Peter the Great would officially declare Russia to be an empire in 1721, by which stage its territory stretched from Finland to the Pacific, and as far south as the Sea of Azov and the northern shores of the Caspian. Only during the following century would the empire gradually expand south and east into central Asia, which would become known as Russian Turkestan (modern Kazakhstan and its Turkic neighbours).

Peter the Great ensured his own survival and that of his Europeanisation programme by curtailing the strong influence of the powerful pro-Slavic Boyars. Amongst other measures, he imposed a prohibitive tax on their beards, which the Boyars regarded as a measure of their rank (junior ranks were only permitted moustaches). By the time Peter III became Czar in 1762, Europeanisation amongst the Russian ruling family had reached extreme limits.

The man who became Peter III was the son of Peter the Great's elder surviving daughter, and he was born in Kiel as Karl Peter Ulrich von Schleswig-Holstein-Gottorp. His wife was the even more Germanic, Princess Sophie of Anhalt-Zerbst. Peter III could barely put a sentence together in Russian, which hardly endeared him to his subjects. However, he proved even more unpopular with his wife, who had him assassinated six months into his reign. Whereupon she herself became Empress of Russia, which she ruled for thirty-four years, becoming known as Catherine the Great.

From the outset, Catherine was determined to follow in the footsteps of Peter the Great. She started by reforming the administration and ordered the building of new cities. Her court would attract European intellectuals of the highest calibre, epitomised by the Swiss Leonhard Euler, one of the greatest mathematicians of all time. Her reign also enabled homegrown talent to flourish, especially the 'father of Russian Science', Mikhail Lomonosov, who was a remarkable polymath. Not only did he write original poetry, but he also made important discoveries in both chemistry and astronomy. It was during Catherine's reign that Russia extended its empire along the shores of the Black Sea, and south along the western seaboard of North America.

By now it was clear that Russia was emerging as a major player on the European scene. So much so that it would attract the attention of Napoleon. Having conquered most of Europe, in 1812 Napoleon launched his revolutionary army on a drive towards Moscow, which he duly captured. But the greatest military tactician of his age had overlooked three basic facts concerning the Russian Empire: its huge expanse, its vast population and its bitter climate. Once again, the inhabitants of Moscow set fire to their wooden city and withdrew to the hinterland, leaving Napoleon to face the Russian winter amidst the ruins. Napoleon was forced to order a withdrawal. His retreat from Moscow back across Europe was to be one of the most bitter defeats in European history, costing the lives of anything up to 380,000 men.

Following Napoleon's defeat at the Battle of Waterloo in 1815, the Russian Czar Alexander I was invited, along with other European statesmen, to the Congress of Vienna. Beside figures of the stature of Metternich, Wellington and Talleyrand, Alexander I sought to shape the future of Europe through the coming century. This was the first time in history that leaders from throughout Europe had met to make such momentous decisions. Where Alexander I was concerned, the Congress of Vienna was a huge success. He managed to gain control of Poland, at the same time ensuring peaceful coexistence in Europe. He also signed a Holy Alliance, a coalition of monarchist powers intended to crush secularist republicanism and revolution. Having begun his reign as a liberal, Alexander I had by now developed into a reactionary nationalist tyrant.

By this period the upper classes in Russia had become completely Europeanised, as described by Tolstoy in *War and Peace*. Yet the serfs, though granted their 'liberation', remained members of a huge downtrodden slavic underclass. These were the lumpenproletariat, described by Marx as 'owning nothing but their labour'. Here we see the opening words of Tolstoy's other great novel, *Anna Karenina*, applied on a continental scale: 'All happy families are alike; each unhappy family is unhappy in its own way.' This 'unhappiness' in Europe remained more or less contained 'in its own way', with cycles of alternating liberation and repression. On the other hand, the Russian way involved ever-increasing autocratic rule, which began transforming Siberia into a vast penal colony, and ensured that no Bohemian or intellectual community in the great cities of Europe was without its cadre of exiled Russian revolutionaries.

By the beginning of the twentieth century, the balance of powers in Europe was assured. It was built on the blueprint set out by the Treaty of Westphalia, with foundations laid down by the Congress of Vienna, and rising on bricks and mortar through the nineteenth century in a series of interlocking treaties. However, all it took was the removal of one brick for the entire house to come tumbling down. This might have resulted in just another self-destructive European war. However, by now the European empires spanned the globe, while the scientific and industrial revolutions had enabled the construction of a monstrous military machine. This meant that instead of a European civil war, like the Thirty Years War, or to a large extent the Napoleonic Wars, by 1914 humanity found itself capable of launching a World War.

By 1917 the Russian army was in a state of collapse, as was the country it was meant to be defending. In March 1917, the weak and unpopular Czar Nicholas II was forced to resign in favour of a Provisional Government. The Germans shipped the exiled Bolshevik revolutionary Lenin back to Russia, in the hope that he would foment a situation that resulted in a Russian surrender. This did take place, but prior to it Lenin had outwitted his political opponents – a majority who ranged from social democrats to fellow revolutionaries – and staged a Bolshevik Revolution. Lenin took charge of the new Revolution, proclaiming a deceptive blend of Marxist, Communist and his own ideas.

A civil war ensued, between the Reds (under Lenin, but led by his henchman, Trotsky) and the Whites (ranging from Czarists to democrats to anarchists, supported by opportunistic invasions by British and American expeditionary forces). Five years later, the Reds emerged victorious, and Lenin decreed that Russia was now the Union of Soviet Socialist Republics. This proved to be neither a union, nor socialist, nor ruled by soviets (workers' committees), or a republic. Instead it was a re-emergence of the Russian Empire in a different guise.

The country was now subject to autocratic rule by a pseudo-Czar – devoid of familial, or indeed any recognised form, of succession. In this, it has been compared variously to the Papacy or a mafia family – where a leader 'emerges'. Just over a year after the civil war ended, Lenin died. Whereupon his expected successor Trotsky fled for his life, and a Georgian named Stalin, who really had been a gangster (and a trainee priest), 'emerged' as leader.

Surprisingly, there was a genuine ideological clash behind this seizure of power. Trotsky subscribed to Marx's slogan, 'Workers of the World Unite', and wished to spread the communist revolution across the globe. Stalin, on the other hand, wished to consolidate 'communism in one country'. Only then would he launch the 'historical inevitability' of communism superseding the various forms of capitalism that had evolved in the 'free world'.

Anyone questioning the *raison d'être* of previous empires had received an answer much like the justification for climbing Mount Everest: 'because it was there'. But now history, too, had become scientific. Ideas took the place of facts. Such was the nature of capitalism that it was historically predetermined to destroy itself, whereupon an entirely new socio-economic age would emerge, where all were equal under the 'dictatorship of the proletariat'. All property would be collectively owned by a classless society. The means of production would be in the hands of public ownership . . . and so on, for three eight-hundred-page volumes of Marx's *Das Kapital.* (He had planned to write six volumes, but managed to convey his message nonetheless.)

For many years people had dreamt of a just society. 'To the Kaiser and Lenin', and so forth. In the Russian Empire, prior to the Revolution, it had been possible to ask: 'What have the Romanovs ever done for us?' But the advent of communism rendered such naive enquiries redundant. Marx had discovered the science that lay behind 'inevitable' history, and science was not open to question.

The class-ridden societies of the West – from country-house Britain to robber-baron America – looked on in horror, fearful that the contagion of communism would spread. In America, the International Workers of the World (the Wobblies) attracted thousands, leading strikes. In 1918, amidst the chaos of defeated Germany, the journalist Kurt Eisner declared Bavaria an independent communist state. Hungary also declared itself communist. In Britain, 60,000 striking Glasgow workers had to be dispersed by tanks, and the Scots revolutionary leader, John Maclean, was appointed from Moscow as 'Bolshevik consul to Scotland'.[44]

In 1921–22, Russia (which became the USSR during this period) would suffer from the Volga Famine. This was caused by the chaos of the civil war, drought and inadequate transportation. Yet it was further exacerbated by Lenin's introduction of War Communism. This entailed

---

44 After his death, Angliyskiy Prospekt (English Avenue) in St Petersburg (then Russianised to Petrograd), would be renamed Maklin Prospekt after the former Scots consul. It has since been returned to its original name.

grain stocks being seized from the peasantry, whom the Bolsheviks saw as resistant to communism, in order to provide for the urban proletariat, whose loyalty was essential.

Insurrection, especially by the sailors at Kronstadt, the naval base outside St Petersburg where the Revolution had begun, led Lenin to soften his rigid policy. Instead, he introduced the New Economic Policy, which permitted, especially in the countryside, 'a free market and capitalism, both subject to state control.' Despite this, five million died in what became known as the Volga Famine, which raged through a large region south-east of Moscow, as far east as the Urals, as far south as the Caspian.

In 1931, seven years after Stalin had succeeded to power, he admitted, with admirable frankness:

> We have fallen behind the advanced countries by fifty to a hundred years. We must close that gap in ten years. Either we do so then or we'll be crushed.

The last remark was not entirely paranoia. Stalin's response to this situation was to abolish the New Economic Policy and instigate the first Five Year Plan. This decreed that all land should be collectivised, and peasants marshalled onto large collective farms. Peasants who resisted giving up their plots of land, or any who had made a profit during the days of the New Economic Policy, were labelled 'kulaks' and decreed 'enemies of the working class'. This insistence on idealism over realism would result in the 1922–23 Ukraine Famine, which saw ten million deaths over a region extending as far as Kazakhstan and beyond.

By now Stalin's suspicions had hardened into genuine

paranoia. Between 1936–1938, this resulted in the Great Purge. The difference between this and the previous mass deaths was that the purge affected the upper echelons of Soviet society – army officers (especially generals), the professions, the intelligentsia, even the secret police who carried out the purge, as well as the usual suspects amongst the lower orders. This resulted in around one million deaths, with many more sent to the gulags – a new network of forced-labour camps in Siberia.

Others were set to work on Stalin's pet projects, such as the White Sea Canal. This was intended to link Petrograd (by now renamed Leningrad) on the Baltic to Archangel on the White Sea. The result was possibly as many as 750,000 deaths (around twice as many as those who died during the entire construction of St Petersburg). The final achievement was a canal that was not deep enough to permit the passage of ocean-going ships, only barges and the smallest coastal freighters.

The period of the Russian Empire's self-inflicted death and catastrophe would come to an end with the advent of the Great Patriotic War (known as the Second World War in the West) against Nazi Germany. Here too the Russian people suffered catastrophic losses, but this time in a cause to which all the democratic Western nations subscribed. An estimated twenty-six million Soviet citizens would die in the conflict, of which eleven million were military personnel. Nazi Germany lost over four million armed forces and some half a million civilians. Japan lost a total of three million, China twenty million, and so it went on.

The twentieth century would see advances such as in no other era of human history, as well as slaughter on a scale that still defies comprehension. There is no doubt that such conflict spurred human inventiveness. On the other hand, there is no denying that at the same time civilisation transformed itself of its own accord. Widespread electrification, the spread of rail transport throughout the world, refrigeration, telecommunications, and countless other benefits were all for the most part spurred on by humanitarian aims (as well as profit).

The end of the Second World War saw the division of Europe into a communist half and a 'free western' half. The Russian Empire was now larger than it had ever been, and its Czar far more powerful than any of his predecessors. In the new communist countries of the Russian Empire, intellectuals sought to combat the repressive regime. Meanwhile in the free West, a large proportion of intellectuals remained more or less overtly in favour of communism. This was particularly the case in France, where the existentialist philosopher, Jean-Paul Sartre, would influence a generation of Marxists. At the same time in Italy and Greece, only covert CIA manipulation ensured that these countries remained 'free'.

For the best part of half a century, the world saw a Cold War, with the two superpowers being the Soviet Union and the United States. These menaced each other with a series of proxy wars (in Korea, Vietnam and other 'third world' countries), as well as a series of more dangerous 'crises' (Cuba, Berlin and so forth). These latter threatened the planet with nuclear war, and the end of civilisation as we know it. Fortunately, a mix of sanity, accident and sheer luck prevailed. (As we have seen, historical research has revealed that these incidents were hair-raisingly close to the edge – closer even than anyone at the time imagined.)

Ironically it was Lenin who had coined the phrase 'voting with their feet'. Yet it was the communists who erected an Iron Curtain across Europe to prevent the inhabitants of their empire from doing just what Lenin described.

After the Second World War, the overseas European empires soon broke up. The Russian Empire, on the other hand, remained in its greatest incarnation until 1989, when the fall of the Berlin Wall marked the end of the Soviet era of the Russian Empire. When the Russian leader, Mikhail Gorbachev, had introduced *perestroika* (reform and democratisation of the Communist Party) along with *glasnost* (openness and freedom of expression), he had no idea of the pent-up forces he was unleashing. On a trip to Lithuania he naively appealed to the locals, and by extension all other Soviet puppet states (or colonies), not to leave the USSR.

In the scramble for the exit, all that was left was the Russian Federation, with the heroic drunkard Boris Yeltsin resisting a coup by hardliners and becoming the next Czar. Yeltsin took the unprecedented step of introducing free elections and privatising state industries, which then fell into the hands of an unscrupulous gang of oligarchs. In 2000, Yeltsin was succeeded by Vladimir Putin, a former low-ranking KGB officer in East Germany. Putin quickly and brutally asserted his control over the oligarchs and indeed any opposition to his rule.

After years in power, his motives of personal gain gradually transformed into dreams of a return to the glory days of the Soviet Union, with authoritarian rule and the Russian Empire as a world superpower. In this, he appears to have made a similar mistake to Gorbachev – imagining that Russia can hold on to a past that is already history. Even so, Russia remains the world's largest country, and continues its incremental expansion and influence. All this, despite its internal disregard for civil rights embodied in any form of Magna Carta, to say nothing of its complementary external unwillingness to recognise the principles of the Treaty of Westphalia.

Sequence

But are such principles so obvious as to be necessary? Is progress towards them inevitable? Is the entire world bound to evolve towards some kind of liberal democracy? And when such a vision is on the brink of realisation, does this herald 'The End of History', as the American political scientist Francis Fukuyama claimed – after the collapse of the Russian Empire left the United States as the world's only superpower. Such questions will be the constant backdrop to the evolution of our final great empire.

The American Empire

When the ever-perceptive Adam Smith published his *Wealth of Nations* in 1776, he was only obliquely correct in his forecast for America. He did not foresee its independence, let alone that this would take place in the same year as the publication of his masterpiece. On the other hand, he did forecast America's greatness. One day, he predicted, the centre of the British Empire would shift to the New World.

In that same year, 1776, Thomas Jefferson would write the United States Declaration of Independence. In this, he took account of some of the finest philosophical thinking of the Age of Enlightenment. Thomas Paine, John Locke, Jean-Jacques Rousseau, David Hume . . . one could not have asked for a finer pedigree. Or indeed a more heartening and resounding document:

> *We hold these truths to be self-evident, that all men are created equal, that they are endowed by their Creator with certain unalienable Rights, that among these are Life, Liberty and the pursuit of Happiness . . .*

Unfortunately, this stirring vision did not apply to the indigenous Native Americans *or* the transported Africans who were already enslaved in all thirteen states. Indeed, by this time the State of Virginia held over 187,000 slaves, while more than 60 per cent of the population of Georgia were slaves (1770 figures). That said, the British who belatedly tried to win back the American colonies, even going so far as to burn down the White House in 1814, were not fighting for the release of slaves. Neither were the French, who helped drive out the British in the first place: their age of 'Liberty, Equality, Fraternity' still lay thirteen years in the future at the time of American Independence.

But to return to the Declaration in all its glory. It is no accident that these 'self-evident' words resemble mathematical axioms (as in the philosophy of the Jewish-Dutch pantheist – or atheist – Spinoza, in this aspect an unacknowledged influence). Upon such axioms can be built abstract truths extending far beyond their basic origins. Indeed, the growth of America can be seen in this mathematical metaphor. The huge structure that today is encompassed in the idea of Western liberal democracy assumes the truth of Jefferson's initial vision.

To Americans – and to a varying extent their allies, and the entire free world – the deductions from these self-evident foundations are the way society ought to be. They are viewed as a moral imperative. And societies that deviate from such foundations are viewed as evil. As in Reagan's description of Russia as an 'evil empire'. As in Roosevelt's characterisation of the Nazis as 'an enemy of all law, all liberty, all morality, all religion'. As in General Miller in the film, *In the Loop*, describing war: 'Once you've been there, once you've seen it, you never want to go again, unless you absolutely fucking have to . . . It's like France.'

Thus, the 'American Way' – in a country where all its citizens (bar the Native Americans) are ultimately descended from immigrants, the majority less than three generations away from the 'home' country. This accounts for why Americans, on the whole a friendly outgoing people, will frequently reveal to a foreigner within the first few minutes of conversation:

1. How American they are (and you are not!).
2. How Irish/Jewish/Turkish, etc. they are.

There is no conflict in this apparent illogic. Patriotism is unabashed and far stronger than it is in most Old World countries, and it has to be, coexisting as it does with deep 'ethnic' loyalties, largely from the Old World. This must constantly be borne in mind when discussing the American Empire. Even before America was a nation, the participants in the Boston Tea Party dressed as Native *Americans* (even if they did refer to them as Red Indians).

As with the British in the nineteenth century, many say that if anyone had to be top dog in the twentieth century, it was probably best that it was the Americans. Naturally, as in the British case, there have been grotesque blunders. Yet the Americans nonetheless prevailed – most notably tipping the balance in two world wars, assuming the role of world superpower in facing up to the Soviets, and in spreading their popular culture across the globe. Many resented, and looked down upon this 'Coca-Cola' culture, yet there can be no denying that it was popular, in both senses of the word. It was in no sense highbrow or elitist, and a lot of people liked it.

This is the nation that gave the world not only Coca-Cola, but Hollywood films, hamburgers, chewing gum, and the general razzmatazz that accompanies American presidential elections and other great sporting events. No other nation would presume to stage an annual 'World Series' between two of its own teams.[45]

Coca-Cola culture spread throughout the world.

45 I stand corrected. The Canadian Toronto Blue Jays are the only international team to have taken part in (and twice won) this 'world' event.

American presidential elections, and their product, are the modern incarnation of Jeffersonian democracy. Enough said, where the present is concerned.[46] Yet it is worth bearing in mind that even the noble Jefferson himself found it necessary to pen *Notes on the State of Virginia*. According to US expert on human behaviour, Lee Alan Dugatkin, this work was 'written in reaction to the views of some influential Europeans that America's national flora, fauna, including humans, was degenerate.'

Closer to the truth than mere prejudice on this topic is the insight of the nineteenth-century American philosopher, Thomas Dewey. It was he who understood that despite all its inequalities, American life is infused through and through with the *ethos* of democracy. Dewey recognised that 'democracy is more than a form of government; it is primarily a way of associated living . . . of communicated experience.'

America is a nation where 'the individualistic ideal' co-exists with an exaggerated acclaim for success. The French revolutionary slogan 'Liberty, Equality, Fraternity' (which remains its national motto to this day) is a contradiction. Liberty eventually outruns equality. The American way of life acknowledges that fact. Even if we all begin at the same starting line, someone is going to win the race. And America won in the twentieth century. Winners are seldom popular. I remember as a student travelling through Europe, where I was asked by an American student, 'Why do they all hate us Americans so much?' I could only reply, 'Last century it was us British who ruled the roost, and were heartily despised all over the world for this achievement. Now it's your turn.'

---

46 At the time of writing, this 'product' is President Trump.

Which brings us to the question: What exactly is the American Empire? In 1776, the thirteen states that had declared independence stretched in a continuous line down a thousand miles of the eastern seaboard from Maine to Georgia. These extended into the hinterland for an average of 200 miles or so, sometimes much more, sometimes much less. To the north lay eastern Canada, recently taken by the British from the French, which had expanded to include the entire region of the Great Lakes, as well as the hinterland territory now occupied by Ohio, Illinois, Michigan and more.

West of those founding states further down the Atlantic seaboard lay the vast expanse of French Louisiana, stretching north-west from New Orleans up into what is now Canada, in a vast belt of land that was up to 800 miles wide. To the south lay Spanish Florida. The rest of the territory now occupied by mainland USA belonged to Spain, including the region occupied by modern California, New Mexico and Texas. Meanwhile Alaska and the coast-line stretching south for over 500 miles belonged to the Russian Empire.

The original thirteen states had an aggregate population of some 2.5 million, including slaves and Native Americans living within their boundaries. This occupied a territory far less than a tenth of the present USA. The Russians regarded Siberia and Alaska as part of their empire. The westward expansion of the US is regarded as adding to its territory. What is the difference here? Purely one of attitude, it would seem. Both expansions involved the disruption or displacement of indigenous peoples, replaced by settlers (or colonists). But there was one essential differ-ence. The United States actually bought two large chunks of its territory.

In 1803, Jefferson bought the entire Territory of Louisiana from Napoleon for $15 million. In present terms, this is worth anywhere between $300 million and $1.2 trillion, dependent upon which federal agency does the calculation. This may have been a bargain, but it still represented a considerable sum, and Napoleon needed the money at once to fund his wars in Europe. Only one snag: America simply didn't have that sort of money. But Jefferson recognised this purchase for what it was: the making of a future great nation.

So he turned to Barings Bank in London, who facilitated the payment, using their financial expertise. A third of the money would be paid in American gold. Barings persuaded Jefferson that the rest could be financed by government bonds – the very first securities issued by the American government on the international market. Barings now sat down with the French and agreed to purchase these bonds from the French government in return for cash. Barings would then sell the bonds on to buyers on the markets of London and Amsterdam to recoup their outlay (and, of course, make a profit).

It was a risk, but finance involves such risks. Were people willing to believe in the future of America to the extent that they would trust them to pay interest on these bonds, and in ten years or so buy them back? The way this was presented by Barings, any purchaser was in a win-win situation. The Louisiana Purchase, as it now became known, doubled the size of this new nation. The bonds were soon snapped up: people were beginning to believe in America. (Even if nine years later, the British burnt down the White House and tried to take America back.)

Just over half a century after the Louisiana Purchase,

the US secretary of state William H. Seward would buy another huge chunk of land for America. In 1867, he bought Alaska from the Russian Empire for $7.2 million. The Russians needed this to pay for the Crimean War, yet American finances were in an even greater mess, having barely recovered from the Civil War. This purchase of unexplored territory was greeted with derision, and became known as 'Seward's Folly'. But Seward's strategic instincts were right. The Alaska territory was in danger of falling into the hands of the British.

However, unlike the Louisiana Purchase, Seward's strategic victory was a financial loss. His outlay in terms of present-day dollars is still below the balance of cash the federal government has received from Alaska in the 150 or so years since it was bought. Contrary to contemporary wisdom (both within and outside the US), money is not everything – even where America is concerned.

By this time, the United States had taken California from Mexico (1847). Texas had also thrown off Mexican rule in 1836, but it decided instead to become an independent republic. This lasted for ten years, before Texas was annexed by Congress. Then in 1861, there began the most traumatic internal event in the history of the United States. This was the American Civil War, which would last from 1861 to 1865. The mainly rural South employed slaves on its cotton plantations, while all the states of the more industrialised North had abolished slavery by 1804. Things came to a head when the Confederate States of the South threatened secession from the Union, and war between the two broke out.

This was the earliest mechanised war in the world, with both sides using such advanced weapons as repeating rifles, machine guns (Gatling gun), metal-clad ships and even submarines. It was also the first industrialised war, with efficiency increased by the factory manufacture of weapons, technological advances such as railway trains for rapid transport, and telegraph for speedy communications, as well as manned balloons for reconnaissance. The result was a total death toll of around 700,000 – more than the combined US losses in all conflicts, including two world wars, for another century. Not until the Vietnam War would this figure be exceeded.

The Unionist North defeated the Confederate South when General Robert E. Lee finally surrendered to General Ulysses S. Grant on 9 April 1865. Five days later, President Abraham Lincoln would be assassinated by John Wilkes Booth, a Confederate sympathiser. During the Civil War, Lincoln had delivered his famous Gettysburg Address, which to this day is seen as a defining statement of American national purpose. This harks back to the Jefferson Declaration, with Lincoln's ringing words stating that America was a nation 'conceived in Liberty, and dedicated to the proposition that all men are created equal'. He was speaking in November 1863 after the Unionist victory in the bloody three-day Battle of Gettysburg. Here more than 23,000 Union soldiers (and many more Confederates) had lost their lives, and Lincoln resolved:

> . . . that these dead shall not have died in vain – that this nation, under God, shall have a new birth of freedom, and that government of the people, by the people, for the people, shall not perish from the earth.

It is salutary to compare this speech with the Communist

Manifesto, written some fifteen years previously by Marx
(and Engels), coinciding with the widespread European
revolutions of 1848. Marx's address stresses the conflict
between classes, and urges the workers of the world to
unite. Lincoln's address, by contrast, exhorts a free people
to govern themselves.

There is no denying that, even then, America had its
class divides. (To say nothing of the racial divide that had
given rise to the civil war.) However, Lincoln's address is
to a new people, in a new land. The great majority of these
people had not achieved their freedom by revolution, but
by crossing the Atlantic in immigrant ships. Twenty-one
years later, the Statue of Liberty would proclaim: 'Give me
your huddled masses . . . yearning to be free.' America was
a fresh start for those who set foot on its shores. Here is
where Dewey's ethos of democracy differs so radically from
'the dictatorship of the proletariat'.

But America was no utopia, even for those who fled the
Irish Famine, the Jewish pogroms of Eastern Europe, the
poverty – for those ambitious individuals keen to throw
off the shackles of European society, as well as the fugitives
and the ne'er-do-wells. The erection of the Statue of Liberty
would also see the era of the 'robber barons'. Powerful and
ruthless capitalist moguls, who would exploit those same
huddled masses in their factories. Cornelius Vanderbilt,
Andrew Carnegie, J.P. Morgan, Henry Ford and others,
built up huge commercial empires – ruining all competitors
who stood in their way, as well as using the latest innovations and business efficiency, to accumulate fortunes. These
were the pitiless men who made America great, but at great
cost to others.

The government – 'of the people, for the people, by the

people' – would do its best to stand up to these 'barons', whose power often seemed to dwarf that of the government and the law. As J.P. Morgan brazenly informed a judge: 'I don't know as I want a lawyer to tell me what I cannot do. I hire him to tell me how to do what I want to do.'

Yet there was another side to such men. Not once, but twice, this same J.P. Morgan would personally rescue the United States. In 1895, he bought sufficient gold to rescue the dollar by keeping it on the gold standard. And in 1907, he stepped in with a financial guarantee that single-handedly averted a Wall Street crash. The government learned from this. No one should have such power, even if he wielded it for the good. In response, the government eventually set up the Federal Reserve.

Henry Ford invented the modern assembly line at the Detroit factory that built the first affordable 'people's car': the Model T Ford, affectionately known as the 'Tin Lizzie'. As Ford put it: 'You can have any colour you want, as long as it's black.' The American love affair with the automobile had begun. When Rockefeller monopolised the oil business, the government prosecuted him under the Sherman Anti-Trust Act. Rockefeller fought every which way, swapping his companies from state to state, but in 1911 he was finally forced to split up Standard Oil into thirty-two companies. Some of these remain to this day, such as Chevron, and Exxon Mobil.

America was becoming the greatest country on earth, while nobody else noticed. And its empire was itself. America was, and would essentially remain a world *power*, rather than an empire. In those early days it didn't invade countries, or not often. In 1836, the new state of Texas was threatened by Mexico, so the US invaded Mexico. Within two years Mexico was defeated, and the US-Mexico border was redrawn to include New Mexico, Utah and all of California, as part of the United States. (These were new states, not colonies.) In 1902, the US liberated Cuba from the Spanish Empire. Cuba became independent, but only so long as it behaved itself.

In 1903, the US bought out the bankrupt French attempt to build a canal across the Panama isthmus, then a part of Colombia. This was arguably the greatest engineering project undertaken to date, and would be completed by 1914.[47] The Panama Canal's 51-mile stretch of waterway and giant locks created a vital trade link between the east and west coast of North America. Consequently, Washington decided that this valuable trade link should be protected by the United States army occupying a 'canal zone', extending five miles or so on either side of the canal itself.

---

47 Not since the building of the pyramids almost 4,500 years previously had humanity accomplished such a prodigious feat. And not until the Soviets launched the first Sputnik forty-three years later in 1957 would such a purely engineering feat be surpassed. It is no exaggeration to claim that the exponential speed of humanity's historical progress is reflected in the condensed gaps between these three dates. A feat that almost defies belief, yet is reinforced by personal anecdotal evidence.

My father was just eleven years old when the Wright brothers first managed to coax their fixed-wing, chain-driven-propeller contraption almost ten feet into the air for twelve seconds at a speed of almost seven mph to cover 120 feet. My father would have another sixteen years to live when Neil Armstrong first set foot on the moon. Yet it is necessary to repeat that, during this same century, humanity achieved the rather less positive scientific feat (incorporating comparable engineering expertise) of first splitting, and later fusing, the atomic nucleus, with the potential for putting a full stop to this long and superlative history of progress.

This was defined as 'unincorporated territory of the United States', rather than a colony.

The entry of the United States into the First World War would tip the balance in favour of the four leading Western allies (Britain, United States, France and Italy). As a result, at the Versailles Peace Conference, President Wilson was widely recognised as the senior arbitrator amongst the four leading statesmen (which became three, when the Italian leader, Vittorio Orlando, burst into tears and flounced off home when he could not get his way.) Wilson was filled with good intentions, the only American president ever to hold a PhD, and this was the first occasion when it was conceded that America was now probably the world's leading power.

Despite this, Wilson was outwitted by the practised political deceit of the British Prime Minister, David Lloyd George, and the French President Clemenceau. The thirty-five-year-old economist Maynard Keynes, a junior member of the British delegation, resigned in disgust to dash off *The Economic Consequences of Peace*, which became a best-seller, sympathetically received by the informed public and future statesmen throughout the world.

Yet nothing was done about the final treaty, which saddled Germany with crippling debts, and drew arbitrary lines in the deserts of the Middle East, marking out new countries divided between French and British interests. The former blunder would contribute in large part to causing the Second World War. The consequences of the latter blunder remain with us to this day.

America now entered the 'Roaring Twenties' of the Charleston, bootleg liquor and Charlie Chaplin – as well as great parties thrown by the likes of the fictional Great

Gatsby. In America, everything was great. The great party of the 1920s was followed by the Great Crash of 1929, which in turn led to the Great Depression. During this time, skyscrapers began to create the great New York skyline. (Started before the Great Crash, there was nothing left to do but complete these skyscrapers regardless.)

In order to alleviate the effects of the Great Depression, President F.D. Roosevelt introduced the New Deal, a Keynesian-style project designed to put unemployed Americans back to work. Roads were laid out across the country, great projects such as the Grand Coulee Dam were initiated, schools and hospitals were built, even writers were set to work recording the history of states and territories throughout the country, providing a 'self-portrait of America'.

Such was the power of the American economy that the Great Depression affected the entire world. In America, this downturn only came to an end when the US finally abandoned its isolationist policy with a vengeance and embarked wholeheartedly on the war effort, when it entered the Second World War. This was occasioned in December 1941 by the surprise Japanese bombing of Pearl Harbor. The Japanese Admiral Yamamoto, one of the few sceptics of Japan's dream of oriental hegemony, warned: 'We have woken a sleeping giant.' Simultaneously, Hitler, a master of disastrous decisions, excelled himself by needlessly declaring war on America. A beleaguered Churchill drank champagne with his cabinet: Europe was saved, the war would now be won by the allies.

The cost in lives of this war was barely imaginable, let alone measurable. Vague estimates reach 150 million; almost four times more than in the First World War. Europe, Japan and much of China were left in ruins. The transition of power in Japan was masterfully handled by General MacArthur, who effectively became Emperor of much of East Asia. (It would be six years before megalomania caused the corncob-pipe-smoking general to be relieved of his post during the Korean War.)

Western Europe would be rescued by the munificence of the Marshall Aid programme. Stalin, who now ruled Eastern Europe, refused this 'capitalist bribe'. Marshall's $12 billion (well over ten times that amount in present values) rebuilt European commerce, and once again American Coca-Cola, Hollywood, Ford Motors and the like all had a thriving export market. Meanwhile the world's two new superpowers (the USSR and the USA) embarked upon a series of 'proxy wars' – featuring the Korean War (1950–1953) through to the Vietnam War (1955–1975) and beyond.

It was during this period that America elected a president who epitomised his nation in a similar fashion to the way Julius Caesar had epitomised the Roman Empire. This was John F. Kennedy – though the parallels in his actual life are more in keeping with the equivocal Gatsby than Caesar. When the charismatic, youthful and articulate Kennedy took office in 1961, he embodied the hopes of an America that unquestioningly assumed its greatness, yet felt itself once again to be a young optimistic country. 'Ask not what your country can do for you – ask what you can do for your country,' Kennedy declared at his inauguration. Kennedy made it plain that he would champion black civil rights at home, and freedom from communist oppression abroad.

At home, amidst marches, mayhem and murder, the

southern states were in open revolt. At his first summit conference in Vienna with the tough, brash communist leader Nikita Khrushchev, Kennedy was humiliated. The recent fiasco of the US-backed Bay of Pigs invasion of Cuba, growing confrontations over Laos (a prelude to the Vietnam War), and the Soviet threat to swallow up isolated Berlin, proved unanswerable. 'He beat the hell out of me,' confessed Kennedy.

Yet a year later, it was Kennedy who deftly and calmly faced down Khrushchev over the Cuba crisis. And in the same year, in response to the Soviets' superiority in space, he boldly announced that within a decade America would reach, and land on, the moon: 'Not because they are easy, but because they are hard.'

The boyish, energetic image that Kennedy presented, accompanied by his attractive, multi-lingual, Vassar-educated wife Jackie, clad in her scrupulously fashionable outfits, captured hearts around the globe. The White House, which hosted diplomatic soirees and sophisticated cultural events, became known as 'Camelot', after King Arthur's legendary court.

Yet behind Kennedy's Dorian Gray picture lay another darker portrait – every bit as ambiguous as Gatsby's past. Kennedy's father Joe had as good as bought the election for his son, using the vast fortune he had accumulated on the stock market, and allegedly from bootlegging during Prohibition. He had mafia contacts, retained fascist sympathies (he once tried to meet Hitler), and later supported the fanatical anti-communist witch-hunt by Senator McCarthy.

John F. Kennedy appears to have remained for the most part innocently unaware of this. Yet the healthy, poster-boy president was also not quite what he seemed. For years he had been racked by crippling illnesses, including hyper-thyroidism and a rare endocrine disorder (Addison's Disease). Treatment required a constant cocktail of drugs and injections, which brought on hypertension, mood swings and sexual addiction. As he confessed to the bemused, upper-class British Prime Minister Harold Macmillan: 'If I don't have sex every day, I have a head-ache'. This practice ranged from call girls (covertly shipped into the White House when Jackie was away) to the likes of Marilyn Monroe, Marlene Dietrich, and more danger-ously, Judith Exner, mistress of mafia boss Sam Giancana. Distressing though it is to record such a fact, there is no doubt that Kennedy's assassination in Dallas in 1963 came just in time. A wave of shock and grief swept the Western world: there is now a JFK Boulevard in major cities throughout all continents. Even a tearful Khrushchev declared Kennedy's death to be: 'A heavy blow to all people.'

Just over a quarter of a century later, the Soviet Union would collapse, leaving America as the sole superpower. Liberal democracy was the ultimate form of successful government, and under the aegis of the United States, it would inevitably spread throughout the world. Meanwhile America, acting as the 'world's policeman', would aid this evolution. Invasions of Iraq, Afghanistan, Somalia, and even the tiny Caribbean island of Grenada, have proved such dreams to be an illusion.

America, which never had an empire, could thus not lose one. Yet its substitute for territorial colonialism – its power – is undoubtedly under challenge. And ironically this chal-lenge comes from the very source that it assumed it had eradicated. Namely, communism – this time in its new variant forms in China and Russia. Capitalism, it seems, is not the only way of doing things that is capable of survival through self-transformation. Yet for the time being, Uncle Sam remains the world's dominant relative. Just.

Future prospects

'There's many a slip 'twixt the cup and the lip' – a proverb that has held true for more than two millennia. Several decades ago, it was 'inevitable' that Japan would become Asia's leading economic powerhouse. Now it is China's turn. Similarly, 'the end of capitalism' has been predicted since we first recognised its existence – generally agreed to have been around 500 years ago. Yet still it persists, in its latest adaptive form. This was the economic engine that lifted much of the world out of poverty, at the same time exploiting most those who benefitted from it least.

According to the biblical adage attributed to Christ: 'The poor are always with us.' So, it seems, are the filthy rich. And contrary to polls, slanted statistics, practitioners of ingenious econometrics and other magi of our age, the worldwide gap between these two strata of society has remained much the same since antiquity.

In 1909, the Italian economist Vilfredo Pareto showed that 'through any human society, in any age or country', 20 per cent of the population owned 80 per cent of the wealth, and 20 per cent of that 20 per cent owned 80 per cent of that 80 per cent, and so on. According to this 80:20 power law, the top 0.6 per cent of the population should own 38.4 per cent of the wealth. According to the January 2019 OECD figures, the top 0.6 per cent of the world's population owns 39.3 per cent of the world's wealth. How to ameliorate this seemingly permanent discrepancy? In a word: tax. Those who cry, 'Socialism! Communism! . . .' should remember that capitalism was most successful during the years following the Second World War, when top rates of income tax in USA and the UK were over 90%. (In 'socialist' Sweden it reached 70%.)

The claim that 'the world is going to the dogs' has a similar lengthy pedigree, being one of the earliest secular inscriptions deciphered from Ancient Egypt. Another unpalatable fact was revealed in the nineteenth century by the English economist, Reverend Robert Malthus, who reluctantly proved that the world's population would inevitably outgrow its ability to feed itself. Yet in the words of Charles Dickens' character, Mr Micawber: 'Something will turn up.'

And so it did. The world learned how to produce more food. No little part in this transformation was played by the great German chemist, Fritz Haber, who discovered how to synthesise ammonia from nitrogen and hydrogen gas, thus revolutionising the manufacture of fertilisers. However, Haber eluded canonisation by also creating poisonous gas for use in warfare.

Humanity's transformations have almost invariably emerged from left field. Accidents (such as Fleming's discovery of penicillin), a pig-headed refusal to accept the 'facts' (Pasteur: 'Chance favours the prepared mind'), as well as the genius flash of inspiration (Archimedes' discovery of the buoyancy principle: 'Eureka!'), and many such discoveries, have all played their part in changing the course of history in utterly unforeseen fashion.

The latest of these life-changers is perhaps the computer-driven IT revolution. Just thirty years ago, people walking down the street talking animatedly to themselves, or believing it necessary to transmit their every passing thought for approval/disapproval by a host of imaginary friends, were liable to be escorted into care for their own good. Now they are simply part of social media.

The latest candidate for 'The End' (the catastrophe that will destroy our planet) is global warming. In my youth, it was a nuclear holocaust: few of us believed we would live until we were sixty. There has always been the argument: 'Ah, but this time it's different.' This expression of wish-fulfilment has most frequently been employed by optimistic well-informed financiers during a prolonged bull market, when faced by nay-sayers predicting a crash that will destroy the world economy.

Democracy is a recipe for short-termism, and such governments are unlikely to implement collectively all the drastic solutions required to reverse global warming. Alternatives for the survival of our species, such as emigration to Mars, are more a matter between Elon Musk and his psychiatrist. Miracles such as cold fusion and massive powerful carbon dioxide absorbents have long been awaited. The saving miracle, if it arrives, will be the biblical cloud 'no bigger than a hand's span', which may even now be materialising just beyond the left field of our vision. As for future great empires, and the world geo-political picture . . . This may not be as harsh as the continuous warfare envisaged by George Orwell in his dystopian novel *1984*; but it is more than possible that he accurately foresaw its empires and their competing spheres of influence. He posited three: Oceania (including the Americas, Australia, southern Africa and Britain), Eurasia (stretching from Portugal to the Pacific) and East Asia (a westward expanded

China). Is it inevitable that one of these will emerge as the dominant power?

A knowledgeable friend of mine once gave me a tip for a two-horse race. The favourite had no chance of winning: place all you can on the other horse. During the race, the favourite fell at one of the early fences, leaving the field clear for our horse. Alas, the weight of expectation on this horse evidently proved too great, for it keeled over with a heart attack within sight of the finishing line. Such is, and always has been, the state of predictions concerning the future of the world and the great empires that will form its history.

Acknowledgements

This book relies in many ways upon all those who have contributed to my education – both formal (schools, universities, books etc.) and confidential (wise words in my ear from sources ranging from senior politicians to an ex-mafia don). Unlike many works of mine, this incorporates a lifetime's experience, along with the opinionated reactions of the one who experienced it.

With regards to the finished product, any opinions, mistakes and so forth should be attributed entirely to the author – and certainly not to any of his confidential advisors. The book itself would not have been possible without the meticulous and ever-helpful editing of the staff at Hodder. In particular, this includes my editors, who switched horses in mid-race: namely Drummond Moir and Ian Wong. Also, all others at Hodder who have been so helpful with my occasional requests.

As ever, I would like to thank my long-term agent Julian Alexander. Also his assistant Ben Clark, who remains ever helpful. I would particularly like to thank the staff at the several libraries and record offices I have consulted both here and abroad, who have provided me with so much helpful information and guidance. And as always, without the unfailingly helpful staff at Humanities 2 in the British Library, this book would not have been possible.

Picture Acknowledgements

Sources and References

I have listed precise citations for the Introduction and Chapter 1, where I have used a large variety of sources. Quotation sources in the later chapters are mostly indicated in the text; others are taken from the Recommended Reading books.

Introduction: Three Telling Tales of Empire

p. 1. 'the oceans of . . .', many sources repeat versions of this phrase, see for instance, Niall Ferguson, *Civilization* (London, 2011), p. 29.

p. 2. 'a king without . . .', see Miles Menander Dawson, *The Wisdom of Confucius* (Boston, 1932), pp. 57–8.

p. 2. 'to proceed all the way . . .', cited cover, Gavin Menzies, *1421* (London, 2003).

p. 3. 'at best circumstantial . . .', Ferguson, *Civilization*, p. 29.

p. 3. 'a number of medieval . . .', Menzies, *1421*, p. 241.

p. 3. 'the Chinese . . . had discovered . . .', see: *Junk History*, ABC Four Corners programme, 31 July 2006, consulted 1.6.2018.

p. 4. 'were hostile to commerce . . .', Christopher Lascelles, *A Short History of the World* (London, 2012), p.65.

p. 4. 'one of the greatest . . .', C. Simon Fan, *Culture, Institution and Development in China* (London, 2016), p. 97.

p. 4. 'for the perpetual prevention . . .', for this and subsequent citations re the Golghar, see for instance Jan Morris, *The Stones of Empire* (Oxford, 2005 ed.), pp. 220–2.

p. 6. 'However, the complexity of . . .', Secret Report LA-602, 'Ignition of Atmosphere with Nuclear Bombs', stamped 'unclassified 7/30/79', p. 18.

p. 7. 'even more dangerous . . .', Alex Wellerstein blog, 'Nuclear Secrecy', cited John Horgan, *Scientific American*, 3 August 2015.

p. 8. 'It was subsequently determined . . .', see Wikipedia entry on Stanislav Petrov, citing as source Channel 4, *1983:The Brink of the Apocalypse*: section on Petrov starts 29.06 mins into programme, consulted 5.6.2018.

p. 9. 'All right . . . all right . . .', original script of *Monty Python's Life of Brian* posted on internet, consulted 5.6.2018.

p. 10. 'An extensive territory . . .', see *Oxford English Dictionary* (Oxford, 1989, 2nd ed.), vol. 5.

Chapter 1: The Akkadian Empire

p. 13. 'During the flooding . . .', Herodotus, *The Histories*, bk 2, p. 97.

p.14. 'two and two of all . . .', Genesis 7: 14–15.

p.16. 'My mother was a changeling . . .', cited Georges Roux, *Ancient Iraq* (London, 1980), p. 145.

p. 16. 'tore down the . . .', et seq, cited Roux, *Iraq*, p. 146.

p. 17. 'dug up the soil of the pit . . .', 'The Chronicle of Early Kings', ABC 20: 18–19.

p. 17. '[Sargon] had neither rival nor . . .', 'The Chronicle of Early Kings' at Livius.org, adapted from Grayson, 1975 and Glassner, 2004.

p. 18. 'washed his weapons . . .', see Amelie Kurt, in *The Ancient Near East* (London, 1995), vol. 1, p. 49.

p. 19. 'who ate bread . . .', cited Mario Liverani, *The Ancient Near East* (London, 2013), p. 143.

p. 19. 'Now, any king who . . .', cited Roux, *Iraq*, p. 149.

p. 20. 'Sargon's daughter made herself . . .', et seq, see Paul Kriwaczek, *Babylon* (London, 2010), pp. 120, 121, 122.

p. 21. 'In his old age all . . .', et seq, cited Roux, *Iraq*, p. 148.

p. 24. 'stylised borrowing on . . .', et seq, see Guy Deutscher, *Syntactic Change in Akkadian* (Oxford, 2000), pp. 20–1.

p. 25. 'The year when Sargon . . .', Kriwaczek, *Babylon*, p. 127.

p. 26. 'units which would remain . . .', ibid.

p. 26. 'bewildered, confused . . .', cited & et seq, see Roux, *Iraq*, p. 150.

p. 27. 'Empires based solely on . . .', Kriwaczek, *Babylon*, p. 159.

p. 28. 'nearly all Palestinian . . .', Stiebing, *Ancient Near East*, p. 77.

p. 28. 'Aerial photographs of . . .', ibid., p. 78.

p. 28. 'The First World . . .', see title *Akkad: The First World Empire*, ed. Mario Liverani (Padua 1993).

p. 28. 'construction seemingly going . . .', Kriwaczek, *Babylon*, p. 129.

p. 28. 'In no case is the . . .', et seq; ironically Liverani's citations come from p. 2 of his title *Akkad: The First World Empire*.

p. 29. 'Up until now civilization . . .', Kriwaczek, *Babylon*, p. 119.

p. 30. 'Herodotus describes the . . .', see Harriet Crawford, *Sumer and the Sumerians* (New York, 1993), p. 85.

p. 32. 'We know that life . . .', H.G. Wells, *A Short History of the World* (London, 1965 ed.), p. 62.

p. 33. 'When you are thinking of . . .', P.J. O'Rourke, *All the Trouble in the World* (New York, 1994).

Chapter 2: The Roman Empire

I have made liberal use of the vast literature devoted to this subject. Here are some titles recommended for further reading:

Mary Beard, *Confronting the Classics* (London, 2013).

Mary Beard, *SPQR: A History of the Roman Empire* (London, 2015).

Luciano Canfora, *Julius Caesar: The Life and Times of the People's Dictator*, trans. Hill & Windle (Oakland, 2007).

Philip Freeman, *Julius Caesar* (London, 2008).

Edward Gibbon, *The Decline and Fall of the Roman Empire* (London, 2010).

Anthony Kamm, *The Romans: An Introduction* (London, 1995).

Tacitus, *The Annals of Imperial Rome*, trans. Grant (London, 1956).

Chapter 3: The Umayyad
and Abbasid Caliphates

Recommended further reading:

Jim Al-Khalili, *Pathfinders: The Golden Age of Arabic Science* (London, 2010).

André Clot, *Harun al-Rashid*, trans. John Howe (London, 2005).

Shirley Guthrie, *Arab Women in the Middle Ages* (London, 2001).

Hugh Kennedy, *Caliphate: The History of An Idea* (New York, 2016).

Hugh Kennedy, *The Prophet and the Age of the Caliphates* (London, 1986).

Jonathan Lyons, *The House of Wisdom* (London, 2009).

C.W. Previté-Orton, *The Shorter Cambridge Medieval History, Vol. 1, Later Roman Empire to the Twelfth Century* (Cambridge, 1979).

Chapter 4: The Mongol Empire

Recommended further reading:

The Secret History of the Mongols, trans. Igor de Rachewiltz (Netherlands, 2006).

Christopher Atwood, *Encyclopedia of Mongolia and the Mongol Empire* (New York, 2004).

Carl von Clausewitz, *On War*.

Peter Jackson, *The Mongols and the Islamic World* (London, 2017).

Frank McLynn, *Genghis Khan: The Man Who Conquered the World* (London, 2015).

Jack Weatherford, *Genghis Khan and the Making of the Modern World* (New York, 2004).

Chapter 5: The Yuan Dynasty

Recommended further reading:

Chan, Hok-lam & W.T. De Barry, *Yuan Thought: Chinese Thought and Religion under the Mongols* (New York, 1982).

Elizabeth Endicott-West, 'The Yuan Government and Society' in *Cambridge History of China*, Vol. 6.

John D. Langlois, *China Under Mongol Rule* (Princeton, 1981).

Ann Pauldan, *Chronicle of Chinese Emperors* (London, 1998).

Chapter 6: The Aztec Empire

Recommended further reading:

Nigel Davies, *The Aztecs: A History* (London, 1973).

Bernal Diaz, trans. J. Cohen, *The Conquest of New Spain* (London, 1963).

Miguel Leon-Portilla, trans. J. Davies, *Aztec Thought and Culture* (Oklahoma, 1978)

Michael Smith, *The Aztecs* (Oxford, 2012).

Jacques Soustelle, *Daily Life of the Aztecs on the Eve of the Spanish Conquest* (Stanford, 1961).

Chapter 7: The Ottoman Empire

Recommended further reading:

Roger Crowley, *Constantinople: The Last Great Siege 1453* (London, 2005).
Caroline Finkel, *Osman's Dream: The Story of the Ottoman Empire 1300–1923* (London, 2005).
Halil Inalcik, *An Economic and Social History of the Ottoman Empire (1300–1600)* (Cambridge, 1997).
Patrick Kinross, *The Ottoman Centuries* (London, 1977).
Philip Mansel, *Sultans in Splendour: The Last Years of The Ottoman World* (London, 1988).
John Julius Norwich, *A Short History of Byzantium* (London, 1998).

Chapter 8: The British Empire

Recommended further reading:

Eric Hobsbawm, *The Age of Empire* (London, 1987).
Ronald Hyam, *Britain's Imperial Century 1815–1914* (London, 2002).
Jan Morris, *Pax Britannica* (London, 1968).
Jan Morris, *Heaven's Command: An Imperial Progress* (London, 1973).
Jan Morris, *Farewell the Trumpets* (London, 1978).

Chapter 9: The Russian Empire

Recommended further reading:

Archie Brown et al, *The Cambridge Encyclopedia of Russia and the Soviet Union* (Cambridge, 1982).

George Freeze, *Russia: A History* (Oxford, 2002).

Robert Service, *A History of Twentieth Century Russia* (London, 1999).

Hugh Seton-Watson, *The Russian Empire 1801–1917* (London, 1967).

Chapter 10: The American Empire

Recommended further reading:

Paul Boyer (ed.), *The Oxford Companion to United States History* (Oxford, 2001).

Mark C. Canes & John A. Garraty, *The American Nation: A History of the United States* (New York, 2015).

William E. Leuchtenburg, *The American President: From Teddy Roosevelt to Bill Clinton* (New York, 2015).

Gordon S. Wood, *Empire of Liberty: A History of the Early Republic 1795–1815* (New York, 2009).

Aristide Zolberg, *A Nation by Design: Immigration Policy in the Fashioning of America* (London, 2006).

Index

An invitation from the publisher

Join us at www.hodder.co.uk, or follow us
on Twitter @hodderbooks to be a part of
our community of people who love the very
best in books and reading.

Whether you want to discover more about a book
or an author, watch trailers and interviews, have the
chance to win early limited editions, or simply browse
our expert readers' selection of the very best books,
we think you'll find what you're looking for.

And if you don't, that's the place to tell us what's missing.

We love what we do, and we'd love you to be a part of it.

www.hodder.co.uk

@hodderbooks

HodderBooks

HodderBooks